Pocket
PHUKET

TOP EXPERIENCES • LOCAL LIFE • MADE EASY

Trent Holden, Kate Morgan

Jul 2013

In This Book

QuickStart Guide

Your keys to understanding Phuket – we help you decide what to do and how to do it

Need to Know
Tips for a smooth trip

Regions
What's where

Explore Phuket

The best things to see and do, region by region

Top Experiences
Make the most of your visit

Local Life
The insider's Phuket

The Best of Phuket

Phuket's highlights in handy lists to help you plan

Best Walks
See the city on foot

Phuket's Best...
The best experiences

Survival Guide

Tips and tricks for a seamless, hassle-free city experience

Getting Around
Travel like a local

Essential Information
Including where to stay

Our selection of Phuket's best places to eat, drink and experience:

◉ **Experiences**

✖ **Eating**

◗ **Drinking**

✪ **Entertainment**

🔒 **Shopping**

These symbols give you the vital information for each listing:

- ☏ Telephone Numbers
- ☺ Opening Hours
- ℗ Parking
- ⊖ Nonsmoking
- @ Internet Access
- 🛜 Wi-Fi Access
- 🍃 Vegetarian Selection
- 📖 English-Language Menu
- 🍴 Family-Friendly
- 🐾 Pet-Friendly
- 🚌 Bus
- ⛴ Ferry
- 🚊 Tram
- 🚆 Train

Find each listing quickly on maps for each region:

Bar Hemingway

16 ◗ Map p233, B2

Legend has it that Hemi
self, wielding a machine
...rate this timber-pan
...ered bar during
...showpiece is a
...en by Papa a...
town. Dress
s.com; Hôtel Rit...
⊙ 6.30pm-2a...

Lonely Planet's Phuket

Lonely Planet Pocket Guides are designed to get you straight to the heart of the region.

Inside you'll find all the must-see sights, plus tips to make your visit to each one really memorable. We've split Phuket into easy-to-navigate regions and provided clear maps so you'll find your way around with ease. Our expert authors have searched out the best of Phuket: walks, food, nightlife and shopping, to name a few. Because you want to explore, our 'Local Life' pages will take you to some of the most exciting areas to experience the real Phuket.

And of course you'll find all the practical tips you need for a smooth trip: itineraries for short visits, how to get around, and how much to tip the guy who serves you a drink at the end of a long day's exploration.

It's your guarantee of a really great experience.

Our Promise

You can trust our travel information because Lonely Planet authors visit the places we write about, each and every edition. We never accept freebies for positive coverage, so you can rely on us to tell it like it is.

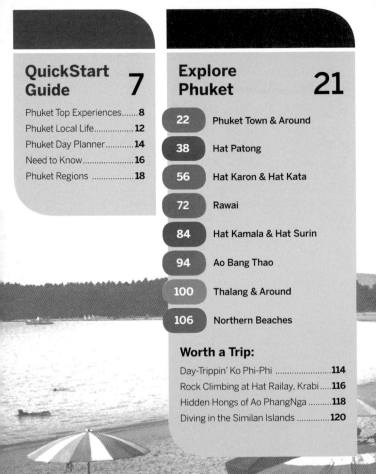

The Best of Phuket **123**

Phuket's Best Walks

Phuket's Best...

Survival Guide **143**

QuickStart Guide

Welcome to Phuket

The original island getaway, Phuket may be older, pricier and not quite as exotic these days, but it's still got it. The white beaches, psychedelic sunsets and aquamarine sea, they're all still here, and Phuket continues to party with the best of them. Sure, it may be too popular for its own good, but that's what happens when you've got it all.

Ao Sane (p79)
LONELY PLANET/GETTY IMAGES ©

Phuket Top Experiences

Big Buddha (p58)

You've seen him peeking out from different angles around the island, but taking in the sheer size of this 45m Buddha statue up close makes for a worthy break from the beach.

GLENN VAN DER KNIJFF/GETTY IMAGES ©

Rock Climbing at Hat Railay, Krabi (p116)

Carry out your *Man vs Wild* fantasy by rock climbing on Krabi's trademark karst formations in Railay. They curve along the coast like a giant limestone fortress.

Diving in the Similan Islands (p120)

Discover the majestic underwater paradise of one of the world's best-known dive spots. You'll be enchanted by everything from tiny plume worms to whale sharks.

TAKAU99/GETTY IMAGES ©

PETER UNGER/GETTY IMAGES ©

Day-Trippin' Ko Phi-Phi (p114)

With its curvy, blonde beaches and bodacious jungles, it's no wonder that Phi-Phi is a popular day trip from Phuket. Spend the day diving, hiking or just lazing around in its azure waters.

Hidden Hongs of Ao PhangNga (p118)

Among these spectacular towering cliffs James Bond's nemesis, Scaramanga *(The Man with the Golden Gun)*, chose to build his lair. Sea kayak around turquoise bays, exploring hidden, peaceful *hongs* (lagoons enclosed by limestone rock).

INGOLF POMPE/GETTY IMAGES ©

MANFRED GOTTSCHALK/GETTY IMAGES ©

Laem Phromthep (p74)

Watch the sun sink into the horizon, turning the sky a deep red orange, from the cape jutting into the Andaman Sea, the island's most-famous viewpoint.

Phuket Local Life

Insider tips to help you find the real Phuket

There are plenty of ways to enrich your holiday when you tire of the beach life. Exploring the old-world charms of Phuket Town is a must, and no trip is complete without at least glimpsing the chaos that is Patong's local nightlife.

Strolling Around the Old Town (p24)

▶ Converted Sino-Portuguese shophouses
▶ Chinese Taoist temples

Often overlooked, Phuket Town is your window into the soul of Phuket, and is the cultural heart of the island. Spend at least a day wandering the streets lined with converted Sino-Portuguese shophouses, where generations-old eateries mix with hip art galleries.

Pub & Grub Crawl Patong (p40)

▶ Seafood stalls
▶ Rockin' bars

Let's face it, Patong doesn't have much of a 'local' flavour as tourism owns this neighbourhood. It does have a particular feel of its own, however, and the best way to experience that is on a pub tour of some of its beer spots that forego the seedy 'sin city' feel and debunk the myth that it's all about girly bars here.

CHRISTER FREDRIKSSON/GETTY IMAGES ©

Phuket Town architecture

Soi Bangla, Patong

Other great places to experience the region like a local:

Wilai (p33)

Phuket Town Markets (p37)

Mae Ubol Market (p49)

Wat Karon (p64)

Wat Chalong (p79)

Rawai's Seafood Grills (p80)

Masjid Mukaram Bang Tao (p88)

Phuket Day Planner

Day One

Spend your first morning de-stressing and getting into holiday mode with a massage and spa at the indulgent **Spa** (p63) in Karon. Head up to the **Big Buddha** (p58) early to beat the heat then grab lunch at **Mom Tri's Kitchen** (p65), taking in the spectacular views you've been waiting for.

Start day one of lazing on the beach at **Hat Kata** (p62) or head over to **Hat Nai Han** (p77). As the sun starts to drop, leave time to make your way to **Laem Phromthep** (p74) for the sunset and views before a cold beer at **After Beach Bar** (p68) on Kata Hill.

Dine right on the beach at Phuket's famous **Boathouse Wine & Grill** (p65). Maybe hold off on Patong till you've settled in, and instead opt for a relaxed beer at **Ska Bar** (p69) or **Rick 'n' Roll Music Cafe** (p69).

Day Two

Wake up and smell the coffee with an espresso at the **Italian Job** (p70), near Hat Kata, then grab a beach lounger at **Re Ká Ta** (p63) and hang around for lunch.

Drag yourself away from the beach and up to the streets behind Hat Surin for some shopping, perhaps beach clothes from **Island Bliss** (p93), beauty products from **Lemongrass House** (p93) or some art from **Soul of Asia** (p93). Enjoy a delicious homemade gelato from **Bocconcino** (p91) before relaxing with a cold drink at **Catch Beach Club** (p87).

Hopefully you've prebooked your show tickets for **Phuket Simon Cabaret** (p51) or **Phuket Fantasea** (p88), but first enjoy a preshow dinner with sunset at **Rockfish** (p90) on Hat Kamala. Then it's time to hit Patong to see what the fuss is all about. Do a pub crawl and bust your moves at **Seduction** (p50), while gay travellers should head to **Backstage** (p50).

Short on time?
We've arranged Phuket's must-sees into these day-by-day itineraries to make sure you see the very best of the region in the time you have available.

Day Three

☼ Nurse your hangover with a greasy, mid-morning cook-up at **Gallery Cafe** (p32), before taking a leisurely stroll around Sino-Portuguese mansions in Phuket Town, or if you're up to it, the guided walk with **Phuket Heritage Trails** (p27).

☼ While you're in Phuket Town, sample its world-class dining at **Blue Elephant** (p29), and hang around for a cooking class to learn all the recipes to take back home.

☾ Head back to Hat Karon for a late-afternoon dip, before freshening up for a low-key barbecue and beer at **Karon Seafood** (p68). Catch a bout of *moo•ay tai* (Thai boxing, also known as *muay thai*) at **Bangla Boxing Stadium**, (p52) before finishing up with a cocktail at the **9th Floor** (p46).

Day Four

☼ Start off in a healthy way with a detox juice at the **Naughty Radish** (p47), and keep the momentum going with a run and a swim on Hat Kamala or Hat Patong. From here you can arrange a paddle on a surfboard, or take a long-tail boat to **Freedom Beach** (p44).

☼ Grab a prawn pizza for lunch at **Bliss Beach Club** (p97) before deciding whether to do the elephant or horse-back safari along the beach. Leave time for a few hours of relaxing on Hat Surin.

☾ Treat yourself to a glamorous evening with a candlelit beachside dinner at **Baan Rim Pa** (p46). And while you're all dressed up, keep it classy with a drink at **White Box** (p50) or **Liquid Lounge** (p92).

Need to Know

For more information,
see Survival Guide (p143)

Currency
Thai Baht (B)

Language
Thai

Visas
Generally not required for stays of up to
30 days.

Money
ATMs are widely available and credit
cards are accepted in most hotels and
restaurants.

Mobile Phones
Local SIM cards are readily available at
convenience stores such as 7-Eleven and
work with any unlocked GSM phone.

Time
Thailand standard time (GMT/UTC plus
seven hours)

Plugs & Adaptors
Outlets usually take the European round
two-pronged pins. Electrical current is 220V.

Tipping
Tips of 5% to 10% for service workers are
greatly appreciated (unless a service charge
has already been included in the bill).

① Before You Go

Your Daily Budget

Budget less than US$50
► Room in a backpackers US$15–30
► *pàt tai* at a street stall US$3
► Beer at a pub US$1.50–3

Midrange US$50–200
► Double room in a decent hotel US$50–100
► Dinner at a restaurant US$15–30
► Massage at a reputable spa US$10–20

Top end more than US$200
► Room at a five-star beachfront resort
US$200–500
► Degustation menu at a top restaurant
$50–100
► Lavish spa treatment at an exclusive resort
US$100–200

Useful Websites

Lonely Planet (www.lonelyplanet.com/thai
land/phuket-province) Destination information, hotel bookings, traveller forum and more.

Jamie's Phuket (www.jamie-monk.com)
A fun insider's blog written by a long-time
Phuket expat resident with excellent photos
and travel tips.

Phuket 101 (www.phuket101.net) Great
photos and loads of ideas for your trip.

Advance Planning

Three months before If travelling in high
season, book your hotel.

One month before Book tickets for Phuket
Simon Cabaret.

One week before Book in for a day at a
beach club.

2 Arriving in Phuket

Phuket International Airport (www.
phuketairportonline.com) is 30km north-
west of Phuket Town. An airport bus (www.
airportbusphuket.com) runs to Phuket Town
(90B, about 20 minutes), or metered taxis
(500B to 600B to most beaches) can be
found about 50m to the right as you exit the
arrivals hall.

✈ From Phuket International Airport

Destination	Best Transport
Patong	Private or metered taxi
Kata & Karon	Private or metered taxi
Kamala & Surin	Private or metered taxi
Rawai	Private or metered taxi, or self-drive

✈ At the Airport

Phuket International Airport There are
ATMs here. You can arrange car hire from
a number of car-rental agencies including
Hertz, Avis and Budget, outside the international arrivals hall. The airport also hosts a
duty-free store as well as a tourist information counter and post facilities.

3 Getting Around

Local transport on the island is much pricier
than in other parts of Thailand. You won't
find metered taxis outside Phuket Town,
while túk-túks and private taxis are unflinch-
ing in their exorbitant prices.

🚗 Private Taxi

An easy way to get around is to hire wheels
with a driver and air-con. A good option if
you're wanting to explore the island on a day
trip (particularly cost-effective if you have a
few people together).

Túk-Túk

Plying the coastal route between beach
towns, this local mode of transport is pricey,
but unfortunately it remains the most
convenient way of getting from A to B.

Sörngtǎaou (Passenger Pick-Up Trucks)

An inexpensive way to get to the beaches
from Phuket Town, but really only an option
if you're not in a hurry.

🚗 Car & Motorcycle Rental

The best way to get around is to have your
own wheels. Scooters can be hired everywhere, but be aware of their dangers; there
are high rates of accidents. Car rental is a
safer option and can be arranged from various parts of the island or at the airport.

Phuket Regions

Ao Bang Thao (p94)
A stunning 8km stretch of blinding white sand with a sprinkling of resorts and beach clubs in the southern half.

Hat Kamala & Hat Surin (p84)
Sophisticated Hat Surin and its slightly more casual neighbour, Kamala, both manage to retain a 'village' vibe.

Hat Patong (p38)
Go-go bars, ping-pong shows, pumping nightclubs and hedonism at every turn: Patong is 'sin city' and proud of it.

Hat Karon & Hat Kata (p56)
Perfect for families, Kata offers high-end dining and beachside bars while Karon has a long stretch of sand.

👁 **Top Experiences**
Big Buddha

Big Buddha 👁

Laem 👁 Phromthep

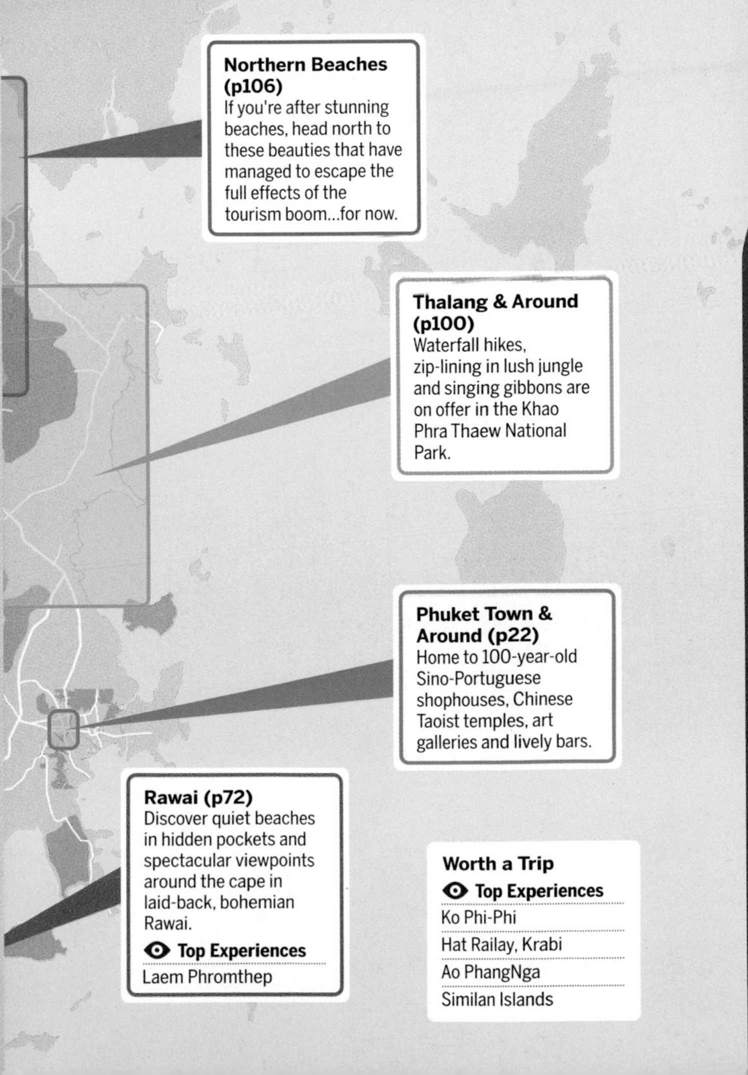

Northern Beaches (p106)
If you're after stunning beaches, head north to these beauties that have managed to escape the full effects of the tourism boom...for now.

Thalang & Around (p100)
Waterfall hikes, zip-lining in lush jungle and singing gibbons are on offer in the Khao Phra Thaew National Park.

Phuket Town & Around (p22)
Home to 100-year-old Sino-Portuguese shophouses, Chinese Taoist temples, art galleries and lively bars.

Rawai (p72)
Discover quiet beaches in hidden pockets and spectacular viewpoints around the cape in laid-back, bohemian Rawai.

⊙ Top Experiences
Laem Phromthep

Worth a Trip
⊙ Top Experiences
Ko Phi-Phi
Hat Railay, Krabi
Ao PhangNga
Similan Islands

Explore
Phuket

Worth a Trip

Hat Kata
LUCA TETTONI/GETTY IMAGES ©

Explore

Phuket Town & Around

What, no beaches? Trade soaking up the sun for soaking up some culture in the island's most authentic corner. Peek down alleyways to find Chinese Taoist shrines shrouded in incense smoke and wander lantern-strewn streets aglow at night. Sino-Portuguese *hôrng tǎa•ou* (shophouses) huddle together, hosting arty cafes, galleries, inexpensive restaurants and buzzing bars, and attracting a hip mixed crowd.

The Region in a Day

☀ Fuel up at **Gallery Cafe** (p32), then take in the old charm of the streets before putting it into context at the **Phuket Thaihua Museum** (p27). Jump in a túk-túk to **Khao Rang** (p27) for city views, shade and fresh air. Opt for some holiday exercise and brave the walk back to town. Hungry yet? Drop into **The Cook** (p31) for a green-curry-chicken pizza.

☀ Dedicate your afternoon to expanding your culinary repertoire at the **Blue Elephant Cooking School** (p27). Otherwise, pick up some art at **Drawing Room** (p35) before grabbing a latte at **Eco Cafe** (p34). Got kids in tow? Head for some underwater fun at the **Phuket Aquarium** (p29) or check out the creepy crawlies at the **Phuket Butterfly Garden & Insect World** (p28).

☾ Dine in royal style at **Blue Elephant** (p29) or enjoy simpler classics at **Raya** (p31) before sipping classy cocktails at **Sanaeha** (p33). Once it gets to 'rowdy o'clock', get over to **Rockin' Angels** (p33) for some cheap beer and live music or **Timber Hut** (p35) for a pub atmosphere.

For a local's day in Phuket Town, see p24.

🔍 Local Life

Strolling Around the Old Town (p24)

💗 Best of Phuket

Drinking & Nightlife

Sanaeha (p33)

Rockin' Angels (p33)

Timber Hut (p35)

Ka Jok See (p35)

Dining

Blue Elephant (p29)

Raya (p31)

The Cook (p31)

Getting There

Airport bus The airport bus to Phuket Town costs 90B and minibus (min 11 people) costs 150B.

🚖 **Taxi** From the airport costs around 500B.

Túk-túk From the beaches to Phuket Town costs around 700B.

Sŏrngtăaou These ply the route from tourist towns along the coast to Phuket Town.

Local Life
Strolling Around the Old Town

The best way to explore Phuket Town is a slow stroll around the Old Town where history seeps out at every turn. This walk takes in some of the Sino-Portuguese relics housing generations-old businesses and restaurants, past shrines and temples hidden down alleyways, to discover local delicacies.

❶ Thavorn Hotel

Opened in 1961, this is one of the oldest hotels still operating in Phuket. Owned by the Phuket Chinese-Thai Thavorn Wong Wongse family, the exterior is now unimpressive but the inside is a throwback to earlier times. There's memorabilia, a grand wooden staircase, a wide lobby and a dusty museum full of tin toys, old movie projectors, historical photos and random junk. It's at 74 Th Rassada.

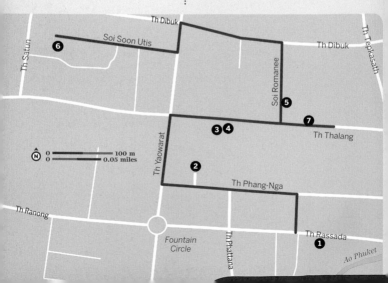

❷ Shrine of the Serene Light

Head along Th Phang Nga, toward the circle where you'll find the **Shrine of the Serene Light** (Saan Jao Sang Tham; ⏰8.30am-noon & 1.30-5.30pm). A handful of Chinese temples inject some colour into the Old Town, but this a cut above the rest. You'll see Taoist etchings on the walls and the vaulted ceiling stained from plumes of incense. From here take a right at Th Yaowarat and right onto Th Thalang.

❸ Oldest Herbs Shop

Crave ginseng or dried insects? You'll find the **Oldest Herbs Shop** (Nguan Choon Tong Herbs Shop; ☎0 7621 5901; 16 Th Thalang; ⏰8am-5pm) (the oldest in Phuket) as you stroll along Th Thalang. Stop here to stock up or to simply watch portions of herbs being weighed on antique scales and mixed ready for sale at this generations-old family business.

❹ Kopitiam

Owned by the same family that runs the Oldest Herbs Shop next door and Wilai (see the boxed text, p33), this narrow converted shophouse has exposed beams, ceiling fans and old black-and-white photos plastered on the walls showcasing the history of Phuket. **Kopitiam** (☎08 3606 9776; 18 Th Thalang) serves inexpensive, and delicious, fare – try the *hokkien mee* or *cha koay teow* (Penang-style stir fried noodles).

❺ Soi Romanee

Turn left off Th Thalang. Once home to brothels, gamblers and opium dens, these days Soi Romanee is as saccharine as a street can get. Located between Thalang Rd and Dibuk Rd, the alley has restored Sino-Portuguese shophouses painted in pretty pastels, fabulous cafes and jazz bars. It's particularly quaint at night when coloured-paper Chinese lanterns cast a dim glow.

❻ Cookie House

At the end of Soi Romanee, take a left on Th Dibuk, another left at Th Yaowarat and right into Soi Soon Utis, where you'll find Mi Han of **Cookie House** (☎0 7621 3010; Soi Soon Utis; ⏰7am-9pm). The young matriarch of this old Sino-Portuguese home, located at the dead end of this tranquil street, makes some mean cookies from freshly pulverised almond paste, egg yolks and butter. They're a flaky and sweet (but not too sweet) Phuket delicacy. Keep them to eat later.

❼ Traditional Roti

Follow your path back the way you came, and from Soi Romanee turn left into Th Thalang. This is your last stop – time to devour one of Abdul's delicious roti. Abdul is a 74-year-old immigrant to Thailand who has been cooking roti on the street in front of his shop for years. Whether you prefer sweet or savoury, this place has it covered, with a sticky banana roti or plain served with a spicy Masaman curry.

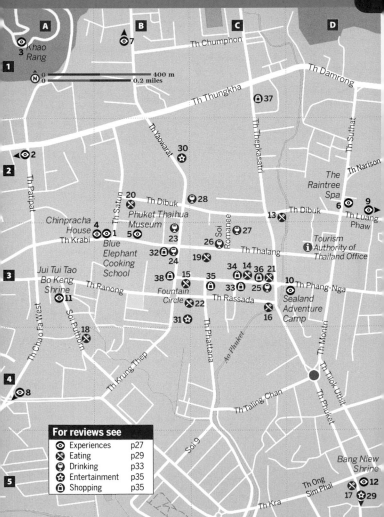

A
B
C
D

1

Khao
Rang
3

N 0   400 m
0   0.2 miles

Th Chumphon

Th Damrong

Th Thungkha

7

37

Th Thepkasatri

Th Suthat

Th Narison

2

2

Th Patipat

Th Yaowarat

30

The
Raintree
Spa

Th Dibuk

28

13

6

9

Th Luang
Phaw

20

Th Dibuk

Phuket Thaihua
Museum

Th Satun

Chinpracha
House

4

1

5

23

27

Soi
Romanee

26

Tourism
Authority of
Thailand Office

Th Krabi

Blue
Elephant
Cooking
School

32

24

19

Th Thalang

3

Jui Tui Tao
Bo Keng
Shrine

11

Th Ranong

38

15

Fountain
Circle

31

22

35

34 14

33

36 21

25

10

Th Phang-Nga

Sealand
Adventure
Camp

Th Rassada

16

Ao Phuket

Th Monthi

Th Tilok Uthit

Th Phuket

Soi Putthon

18

4

8

Th Chao Fa West

Th Krung Thep

Th Phattana

Th Taling Chan

Soi 9

5

For reviews see
◉	Experiences	p27
✕	Eating	p29
⬤	Drinking	p33
✦	Entertainment	p35
🔒	Shopping	p35

Bang Niew
Shrine

12

Th Ong
Sim Phai

17

29

Th Kra

Experiences

Blue Elephant Cooking School
COOKING

1 ◉ Map p26, B3

Once you've dined at Blue Elephant, you'll want to know all of their culinary secrets. Here's your chance. Wow your mates back home with dishes such as *kaeng phed ped yang* (roast duck in red curry), mastered in the grand setting of the restored Sino-Portuguese–style mansion. Half-day classes start at 9.30am and 1.30pm; morning classes include a market visit. Private courses are also available from 5000B per person for four dishes. (☎0 7635 4355; www.blueelephant.com; 96 Th Krabi; half-day classes 2800B)

Phuket Heritage Trails
WALKING

2 ◉ Map p26, A2

Get closer to the charms of Phuket Town with these professional local guides. Discover the hidden symbolism of the town's finest Sino-Portuguese architecture on the Meet the Locals tour (mornings and afternoons; email for details). Foodies will want to take in the Walking Food Tour (Tuesday to Thursday & Saturday) to sample local Phuket favourites and feast on delicacies you might not otherwise find. Prices include meals and refreshments; hotel transfers are included in the Meet the Locals tour. (☎08 5158 9788; heritage.th@gmail.com; 124/1 Th Witchitsongkram; Meet the Locals/Walking Food Tour 2500/1500B)

Khao Rang
VIEWPOINT

3 ◉ Map p26, A1

For a bird's-eye view of the city, head up to pretty Khao Rang, northwest of the town centre. It's at its best during the week, when the summit is relatively peaceful. There are a few restaurants up here with commanding views, making it a pleasant spot for a lazy lunch or sunset drink. A túk-túk from town will cost around 400B return, or go with your own wheels or legs. It's about an hour's walk, but it's not safe to walk at night. (Phuket Hill)

Chinpracha House
MUSEUM

4 ◉ Map p26, B3

Built in 1903, this Sino-Portuguese mansion should be on any antique lovers' list. Others might find it a bit gaudy, maybe even creepy in the bedrooms with their four-poster steel beds and baby cots done up in Victorian lace. But the atrium foyer with its koi pond, the Italian ceramic tiles and historical family portraits are details worth visiting for. The current owners are sixth-generation Thai descendants of the original owner. (Baan Chinpracha; 98 Th Krabi; 100B; ◷8am-4.30pm)

Phuket Thaihua Museum
MUSEUM

5 ◉ Map p26, B3

This flashy museum, formerly a Chinese language school, is filled with photos and exhibits on Phuket's history, from the Chinese migration

Phuket Aquarium

and the tin-mining era to local cuisine. There's also an overview of the building's history, which is a stunning combination of Chinese and European architectural styles including art deco and Palladian, and has a Chinese gable roof and stucco. (www.thaihua museum.com; 28 Th Krabi; admission 200B; ⊙9am-5pm)

The Raintree Spa SPA

6 ⊚ Map p26, D2

These calming lush tropical surrounds are a step up in price and atmosphere from the storefront spas. Skilled therapists don't just go through the motions here. Get silky smooth skin with a sesame body glow (1300B) or indulge in a two-hour tropical-fruit treatment of orange and bergamot

(2000B). (☑08 1892 1001; www.the raintreespa.com; Th Yaowarat; massages from 500B; ⊙10am-9.30pm)

Phuket Butterfly Garden & Insect World GARDEN, MUSEUM

7 ⊚ Map p26, B1

Arachnophobes and entomophobes will want to strike this one off the list. Or perhaps, scoot through the skin-crawl-inducing displays as fast as possible to the fluttery butterfly garden out back. Live fuzzball tarantulas, bird-eating spiders and shiny scorpions are either the coolest things ever, or the stuff of your worst nightmares. Kids, however, will love it all. (www.phuketbutterfly.com; 71/6 Soi Paneung Yaowarat Rd; ⊙9am-5pm)

Phuket Aquarium   AQUARIUM

8 ◉ Map p26, A4

For those who don't have the time or inclination for snorkelling, get an idea of what you're missing out on here. Located at the tip of the Laem Phanwa, there's a varied collection of tropical fish, sharks and other aquatic life – check out the tiger-striped catfish resembling a marine-like zebra or the electric eel with its own voltage meter. (www.phuketaquarium.org; adult/child 100/50B; ◷8.30am-4.30pm)

Feed the Monkeys   ANIMAL INTERACTION

9 ◉ Map p26, D2

Just after crossing over onto Ko Sireh, to the east of town, you'll see a wooden platform with monkey carvings overlooking the mangroves. Inside those mangroves are hundreds of Macaque monkeys. At sunset locals feed them from the platform separated by a small pond. It's a bit of a fun, chaotic scene. Catch a túk-túk from town (500B). (Monkey Platform near the bridge; admission free)

Sealand Adventure Camp   ADVENTURE SPORTS

10 ◉ Map p26, D3

This Phuket Town–based outfitter can put you on the back of an elephant or mountain bike. Or if you prefer, it can put you in a 4WD, or immerse you in a nearby jungle or river on rafting, waterfall and other adventure trips. (☑0 7622 2900; www.phuketsealand.com; 125/1 Th Phang-Nga; trips per day from 1800B)

Jui Tui Tao Bo Keng Shrine   SHRINE

11 ◉ Map p26, A3

This shrine attracts those wishing to bolster their physical health through prayer. It's also a base for serious (read: violently pierced) participants during the Vegetarian Festival (see the boxed text, p36), which makes it a great place to stake out and snap photos like the cultural paparazzi. (Soi Puthon; admission free; ◷6am-6pm)

Bang Niew Shrine   SHRINE

12 ◉ Map p26, D5

Built in 1934, this shrine honours Lao La as principal deity and hosts local Chinese opera productions. (Th Ong Sim Phai; admission free; ◷6am-6pm)

Eating

Blue Elephant   THAI $$$

Royal Thai cuisine in a royal Thai setting – this is one dining experience not to be missed. Set in the beautifully restored Phra Phitak Chyn Pracha mansion (see **1** ◉ Map p26, B3) over stately lawns, everything here is elegant, from the brass cutlery and wooden shuttered windows to the chequered tiled floors and superbly presented dishes. Choose from the set tasting menu or go à la carte, it

Understand

Phuket's History

Phuket's back story reads like an old-school Robert Louis Stevenson adventure novel. It features, among other things, jungle-dwelling pygmies, savvy Indian and European merchants, (supposedly) marauding sea gypsies, immigrant Chinese tin miners, and cross-dressing war heroines (see the boxed text, p105) who helped save Thailand from Burma's imperial lust. It's safe to say Phuket has a past, and has always welcomed foreigners.

Phuket Town was actually founded in the 1st century BC by Indian merchants. Ptolemy, a Greek geographer who visited in the 3rd century AD, dubbed it 'Jang Si Lang', which later became 'Junk Ceylon', the name you'll find on ancient maps of Thailand. Among Phuket's original locals were now-extinct primitive tribes similar to Malaysia's surviving Semang pygmies. Meanwhile, nomads of Malay descent, known today as *chao lair* (also known as *chao leh* or sea gypsies), populated the coastal areas of Phuket. They sailed from cove to cove and island to island in hardy houseboats that could weather the roughest seas, living off shellfish and turtle soup, fishing for pearls and staying until the beach's resources were depleted.

In the 16th century the first of the Europeans descended on the islands, with Portuguese, then French, then British traders arriving for the tin industry. By the early 19th century it was the turn of the Chinese, with thousands of labourers arriving for the tin-mining boom. They brought their culinary and spiritual traditions with them, and when they intermarried with the Thai, a new culture known as the Baba people was born. They built up Phuket Town, erecting enormous homes with Portuguese and Chinese accents, high ceilings and thick walls so they would remain cool. These impressive structures and their Baba inhabitants are the main attractions of Phuket's Old Town.

In the 1970s, beachcombers began arriving en masse, turning the island into one of the world's most famous beach resorts. Tourism remained strong until the tsunami hit on 26 December 2004, killing 250 people on Phuket and 5300 across Thailand – other estimates have it much higher. It was a dark moment in Phuket's history, but things move on and its economy shows no signs of slowing down; development continues at an increasingly unsustainable rate.

Chinpracha House (p27)

doesn't really matter as it's all superb. (📞 0 7635 4355; www.blueelephant.com; 96 Th Krabi; mains 400-1000B; ⏰11.30am-2.30pm, 6.30-10.30pm; 📶)

Raya
THAI $$

13 🍴 Map p26, C2

Unrenovated, unpretentious and un-believably good, things feel authentic and old-wordly at this two-storey Sino-Portuguese gem, with its Chinese cigarette girl posters, gramophone, stained glass and wooden-shuttered windows. Raya has been serving af-fordable Thai fare to Phuket locals for around 20 years – creamy crab meat curry served with rice noodles is the signature dish not to be missed. (Th Dibuk; 200-700B; ⏰10am-10pm)

The Cook
FUSION $

14 🍴 Map p26, C3

The Thai owner–chef here used to cook Italian at a megaresort, so when he opened this ludicrously inexpen-sive Old Town cafe he fused the two cultures. It works a treat. Standouts include the sensational green curry pizza with chicken, or the pork curry coconut milk pizza. You can also get food to take away. (📞 0 7625 8375; 101 Th Phang-Nga; dishes 50-200B; ⏰8am-9.30pm, closed Mon)

Siam Indigo
INTERNATIONAL, THAI **$$**

15 Map p26, B3

Set in a Sino-Portuguese relic and brought to life with chic design and vivid modern artworks, Siam Indigo specialises in Thai cuisine with a French–International twist. While the food doesn't always live up to the hype and the service can be slow, the cocktails gain it extra brownie points and it remains a Phuket Town favourite. (☏0 7625 6697; www.siamindigo.com; 8 Th Phang-Nga; dishes 120-280B; ⏰2-10.45pm)

Gallery Cafe
CAFE **$$**

16 Map p26, C3

After a night of pounding the bars, drag your sorry self down to Gallery Cafe and slump in a comfy couch to browse an extensive menu of alcohol-soaking goodies. All-day eggy breakfasts, pizzas, fat chips with aioli, or perhaps an avocado, feta and vegemite toasty, will do the job nicely. (www.gallerycafe-phuket.com; 106 Rassada Rd; mains 50-200B; ⏰8am-8pm Mon-Sat, to 6pm Sun; 📶)

La Gaetana
ITALIAN **$$$**

17 Map p26, D5

An irresistibly intimate five-table restaurant, La Gaetana has black concrete floors, colourful walls and stemware, an open kitchen in the courtyard and a superb Italian menu including lobster pasta. (☏0 7625 0523; 352 Th Phuket; dishes 210-1800B; ⏰dinner 6-10pm, closed Wed)

Natural Restaurant
THAI **$**

18 Map p26, A4

A Phuket Town staple for more than 20 years, this buzzing restaurant serves up tasty Thai dishes among leafy decor with water features and a clutter of ornaments. It also has lovely rooftop seating. The refreshing dragonfruit juice served in a jar is a great way to quench your thirst after a sweaty day of sightseeing. (☏0 7622 4287; 62/5 Soi Puthorn; 50-150B; ⏰10.30am-11.30pm)

China Inn
INTERNATIONAL, THAI **$$**

19 Map p26, C3

The organics movement meets Phuket cuisine at this turn-of-the-20th-century shophouse. There's red curry with crab, a host of veggie options, tremendous homemade yoghurt and fruit smoothies flavoured with organic honey. (☏0 7635 6239; Th Thalang; dishes 80-250B; ⏰breakfast & lunch daily, dinner Thu, Fri & Sat; 🖉)

Dibuk Restaurant
FUSION **$$$**

20 Map p26, B2

This place is more a marriage of French and Thai than actual fusion; try the whole steamed snapper or frogs' legs in garlic butter sauce. Whichever nation you choose, the food works, and considering its quality and the atmosphere of chandeliers and soft jazz, the price is quite reasonable. (☏0 7625 8148; 69 Th Dibuk; ⏰11am-midnight)

Lotus Steakhouse

INTERNATIONAL, THAI $$

21 🍴 Map p26, C3

A steakhouse with cute white awnings and a turquoise Parisian-style facade is a bit like dressing He-Man up as Barbie. Especially when the 'steaks' here are more white than red (pork, chicken and fish). The real reason to visit is for the inexpensive Thai classics that explode with fresh flavour, and for the fresh fruit juices. (Th Phang-Nga; 60-295B; ⏰9.30am-9pm; 📶)

Brasserie

BELGIAN $$$

22 🍴 Map p26, B3

A good place to splurge on fine food and drink, with serious 700g Chateaubrand tenderloin steaks, lobster bisque and authentic Flemish dishes such as rabbit stew. Get romantic in the Provence-style courtyard or blokey at the wooden bar that serves a great range of Belgian beers along with some joie de vivre. (📞0 7621 0511; www.brasseriephuket.com; 18 Th Rassada ; mains 150-900B; ⏰6pm-late, closed Tue)

Drinking

Sanaeha

BAR

23 🍸 Map p26, B3

If you wanna mingle with Phuket's ubercool crowd, this is where you do it. Sanaeha is a chic bar lit by seashell chandeliers, with plenty of dark corners to sip (tom yum) cocktails and snuggle to a soundtrack of live ambient crooning. Its 'place to be seen' reputation means weekends are packed and table bookings are essential; call at least a day in advance. (📞08 1519 8937; 83, 85 Th Yaowarat; ⏰6pm-late)

Rockin' Angels

BAR

24 🍸 Map p26, B3

Intimate colourful Old Town bar decorated with biker paraphernalia and framed LPs – the Beatles, Cyndi Lauper, the Beach Boys and the Village People are all represented. Weekends can get wild when Patrick, the Singaporean-born owner, jams with his house blues band and whoever wants to sit in. Beers are cold and the crowd is composed of a good mix of Thai and expat locals. (📞08 9654 9654; 55 Th Yaowarat; ⏰5pm-1am)

🔍 Local Life
Eat Like a Local

For local-style eating, **Wilai** (Map p26, B3; 📞0 7622 2875; 14 Th Thalang; dishes from 65B; ⏰10am-4pm, closed Sun) serves Phuket soul food. It does Phuketian *pàt tai* with some kick to it, and a fantastic *mee sua* (noodles sautéed with egg, greens, prawns, chunks of sea bass and squid). Wash it down with fresh chrysanthemum juice.

Eco Cafe

CAFE

25 Map p26, C3

Chiang Mai organic coffee, furniture made from recycled corkboard, an artist's studio and a stack of Nat Geo mags – Eco Cafe is a hipster's dream and would slot in nicely in Portland, Melbourne or Williamsburg. Grab a stool at the window counter and take in the Sino-Portuguese architecture of Th Phang Nga. (Th Phang Nga; ☺10am-6pm; 🛜)

Bo(ok)Hemian

CAFE

26 Map p26, C3

Every town should have a coffee house this cool. The split-level open design feels both warm and cutting-edge. It has wi-fi, used books for sale, gourmet coffee and tea, and damn good chocolate cake. (📞0 7625 2854; 61 Th Thalang; ☺9am-10pm; 🛜)

Glastnöst

CAFE

27 Map p26, C3

There's nothing better on a relentless Phuket Town afternoon than to slip into this cafe (that doubles as a law office) to sip iced Ceylon tea or traditional Phuket coffee, brewed by the lawyer himself. Jazz blares on the sound system and sometimes it's live, if the resident Bossa Nova man is in town. (📞08 4058 0288; 14 Soi Romanee)

LONELY PLANET/GETTY IMAGES ©

Ka Jok See

Casa 104 BAR

28 Map p26, C2

Old Shanghai is born again with burgundy walls, a copper bar and early swing music in the air. (⏿0 7622 1268; 104 Th Yaowarat; ⏱9am-midnight)

Entertainment

Boxing Stadium THAI BOXING

29 Map p26, D5

Moo•ay tai (Thai boxing; also spelled *muay thai*) can be witnessed here twice a week. Ticket prices vary depending on where you sit and include one-way transport. You can get your tickets from **Mark Travel & Service** (⏿0 7622 5741; 19 Th Phang Na). (near the pier; admission general/ringside incl one-way transport 1300/1500B; ⏱from 8pm Tue & Fri)

Timber Hut NIGHTCLUB

30 Map p26, B2

Thai and expat locals have been filling this old clubhouse every night for nearly 20 years. They gather at long wooden tables on two floors, converge around thick timber columns, order red-label whiskey by the bottle to swill at their table, and sway to live cover bands that swing from hard rock to funk to hip-hop. (⏿0 7621 1839; 118/1 Th Yaowarat; admission free; ⏱6pm-2am)

Ka Jok See NIGHTCLUB

31 Map p26, B3

Like Superman and Clark Kent, this place has two identities. It's a restaurant, and a very good one, but once the tables are cleared (akin to the glasses and suit coming off), it becomes a bohemian madhouse party, with super powers. The music bounces between soul, groove, ambient and hip-hop, and has the ability to make even the most severe chorophobes (people with a fear of dancing, really) shake their hips. (⏿0 7621 7903; kajoksee@hotmail.com; 26 Th Takua Pa; ⏱6pm-1am Tue-Sun)

Shopping

Ban Boran Textiles TEXTILES

32 Map p26, B3

Shelves are stocked high here with silk scarves, linen shirts and striped cotton textiles from Chiang Mai, up north. You'll also find Burmese lacquerware and bags that make great gifts and souvenirs. (⏿0 7621 1563; 51 Th Yaowarat; ⏱10.30am-6.30pm Mon-Fri)

Drawing Room ART

33 Map p26, C3

One of the coolest galleries on this art-overloaded strip, Drawing Room has an industrial warehouse feel with concrete floors and roller doors. Interesting affordable works range from metal sculptures to black-marker illustrations and paintings from 3000B to 30,000B. It also holds exhibitions a few times a year. (☎08 6899 4888; 56 Th Phang-Nga; ⏱9am-8pm)

Island Paradise CLOTHING

Set in the same old relic as Siam Indigo, this lovely and expansive hippie-chic boutique (see 15 ✕ Map p26, B3), featuring nothing but up-and-coming Thai designers, has stylishly flowing dresses, silk skirts and blouses, as well as great handbags. (☎0 7625 6418; 8 Th Phang-Nga; ⏱10am-9pm)

Wua Art Gallery ART

34 🔒 Map p26, C3

A funky, artist-owned shophouse featuring faceless, musical, colourful and

bleak oils on canvas crafted by a man known only as 'Zen'. (☎08 0542 5400; www.wua-artgallery.com; 95 Th Phang-Nga; ⏱10am-8pm)

Southwind Books BOOKSTORE

35 🔒 Map p26, C3

Peruse these dusty secondhand stacks to stock up on some paperbacks (remember those?) for your holiday reading material. There are titles in several languages and two branches on this strip. (☎08 9724 2136; 1/2/5 Th Phang-Nga; ⏱9am-7pm Mon-Sat, 10am-3pm Sun)

111 Phuket Art Gallery ART

36 🔒 Map p26, C3

Pick up some psychedelic art featuring local subject matter such as

---

Understand
Vegetarian Festival

Sounds like machine-gun fire fill the streets, the air is nearly opaque with smoke and people traipse along blocked-off city roads, their cheeks pierced with skewers and knives; some have blood streaming down their fronts or open lashes across their backs. No this isn't a war zone, this is the **Vegetarian Festival**, one of Phuket's most important festivals.

Taking place usually in late September or October, the festival celebrates the beginning of 'Taoist Lent', when devout Chinese abstain from eating meat. Shopowners along Phuket's central streets set up altars in front of their shopfronts offering nine tiny cups of tea, incense, fruit, firecrackers, candles and flowers to the nine emperor gods invoked by the festival. Those participating as mediums bring the nine deities to earth by entering into a trance state, piercing their cheeks with an impressive variety of objects, sawing their tongues or flagellating themselves with spiky metal balls.

Beyond the headlining gore, fabulous vegetarian food stalls line the side streets offering a perfect opportunity to sample cheap local treats.

For more info, visit www.phuketvegetarian.com.

Sino-Portuguese buildings covered in overhead power lines, and other interesting pieces. Look out for the three paintbrushes which make up the sign. (111 Th Phang-Nga; ☺9am-8.30pm, closed Sun)

Carat Circle JEWELLERY

37 🔒 Map p26, C1

Peruse cases of rubies, pearls and sapphires. Sure, it has hideous print shirts and cheesy tea sets, but check out those strands of light-bending cultured pearls. Great deals abound. (☏0 7621 2715; 154 Thepkrasattri Rd; ☺9am-6.30pm)

Watcharin Art Studio ART

38 🔒 Map p26, B3

Step inside the swirling mélange of whimsical surrealism where canvasses are stacked and propped up in every available inch of this studio/art library/classroom (formerly Rinda Magical Art). The 30-something owner artists are a joy to chat with when they're not busy teaching up-and-coming art students. (☏08 8386 1449; www.watcharinartstudio.com; 27 Th Yaowarat; admission free; ☺9am-9pm)

Local Life
To Market, To Market

A great way to get a local flavour for a place is to head to the market. **Indy market** (Map p26, B2; www.phuketindymarket.com; Limelight Ave; ☺4-10.30pm Thu & Fri) is a small affair where young Thai hipsters sell cutesy homemade goods – leather purses, soaps, lamps, as well as secondhand clothing. A good spot to pick up some souvenirs. For something larger with a classic 'market' feel, try **Weekend Market,** (off Chao Fa West Rd; ☺late afternoon-10pm Sat & Sun) just outside of town. It's best visited in the evening when things get lively and is a great spot to grab a feed. Otherwise keep things local at bustling **Ranong Main Market** (Map p26, B3; Th Ranong; ☺early-midday), specialising in fresh produce.

Explore

Hat Patong

If Patong were a celeb, it'd be sprawled over the covers of trashy mags daily. It's Charlie Sheen's drug-induced meltdowns, Pammy's boob job and Hugh Grant's indiscretions. Its knack for turning the midlife crisis into a full-scale industry make it rampant with unintentional comedy and the only thing pure is the white sand on the beach. If you wanna party, come to Patong.

The Region in a Day

☀ Nurse that hangover with a morning dip before some silence at **Good Luck Shrine** (p44) or a Thai herbal steam bath at **Let's Relax** (p44). If that sounds a little dull, get behind some power on one of the fat-wheeled Harley bikes at **Nicky's Handlebar** (p44) before a fresh Thai lunch at **The Orchids** (p47).

☀ Escape the buzzing jet skis and the afternoon hordes by hopping in a long-tail boat for **Freedom Beach** (p44) or head to **Ao Sane** (p79) for some peaceful sunbathing.

☾ As night rolls around, Patong kicks into action so if you don't have tickets for **Phuket Simon Cabaret** (p51) or *moo•ay tai* at **Bangla Boxing Stadium** (p52), the bars and clubs will keep you busy. Dine at swanky **9th Floor** (p46) for city views before you hit the sin-city epicentre that is Th Bangla, and the dance floor at **Seduction** (p50).

For a local's day in Patong, see p40.

🔍 Local Life

Pub & Grub Crawl Patong (p40)

♥ Best of Patong

Dining
9th Floor (p46)

Baan Rim Pa (p46)

White Box (p47)

Nightlife
Seduction (p50)

Factory Bar (p51)

Sound Phuket (p52)

Getting There

🚖 **Taxi** Private taxi from the airport will cost around 650B.

Minibus A minibus (min 11 people) from the airport costs 150B.

Sŏrngtăaou From Phuket Town costs 30B.

Local Life
Pub & Grub Crawl Patong

One night in Patong is obligatory for any trip to Phuket. And while bar girls playing ping pong – without paddles – may not be your thing, you can still have a good time taking in the spectacle of Th Bangla and hitting some bars and pubs along the way. This walk takes in some of the less, er, sordid spots to fill up on beer and booze.

❶ Monte's

Start with a few cold beers at this casual tropical pub. **Monte's** (Th Phisit Karani; ⏱10am-1am) has a thatched roof, a natural-wood bar, dozens of orchids and a flat-screen TV for sport. Perfect for easing into a big night. Once it's time to move on, head down the hill on Th Phisit Karani and turn right onto Th Rat Uthit. Follow this main street for about 500m, checking out the rows of seafood restaurants.

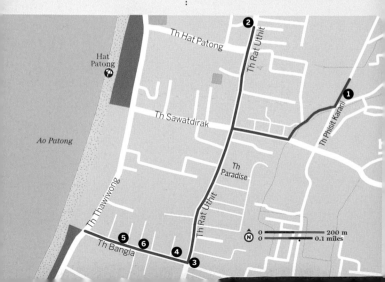

❷ Patong Food Park

Continue on Th Rat Uthit for a few minutes past Th Hat Patong and you'll find **Patong Food Park** (Th Rat Uthit; ⏱4pm-midnight) – a local foodie's dream world – on your left. There's fresh fish, crab, lobster, roasted pork leg, satay and *sôm•đam* (spicy green papaya salad) carts. All cheap and delicious. There's a reason it's always packed with locals and expats. Grab a snack here to line your stomach.

❸ Rock City

From Patong Food Park, head back the way you came along Th Rat Uthit, and follow the street straight down, where you'll notice things start to get noisier and rowdier. On the corner of Soi Bangla and Th Rat Uthit is your next drinking spot, **Rock City** (www.rock cityphuket.com; Th Rat Uthit; ⏱8pm-4am). Limber up your neck in preparation for some serious headbangin' to '80s rock and metal. This dark den lives on the glory of AC/DC, Metallica and Guns N' Roses tribute bands attracting a rockin' crowd of tourists and locals. Get stuck into some rocktails to prepare yourself for Th Bangla.

❹ Thanon Bangla

Straight out the doors of Rock City and you are here. For some visitors, Th Bangla *is* Patong – tales of go-go bars, ping-pong shows, ladyboys and debauchery are the drawcard. For others it's simply a one-night experience before making a retreat to their beachside resort. The street is Patong's beer and bar-girl mecca and features a number of spectacular go-go extravaganzas, where you can expect the usual mix of bored-looking gyrating Thai girls and often excitable red-faced Western men. That said, on the surface the atmosphere is more carnival than carnal or carnage, attracting a mix of tourists and genders. Do a few laps to let it soak in,

❺ Aussie Bar

It may be an Aussie-themed bar, but Patong's **Aussie Bar** (⏱9am-3.30am; 📶) is pretty darn good after you've had enough of Bangla's street circus. You might be on holiday but there's no need to miss the footy, V8 supercars, cricket, soccer etc when you've got eight large sports screens beaming it in. Get competitive on the pool tables or foosball, or just do some elbow exercises at the bar with a VB. You bewty!

❻ Bangkok Burger Co

A few doors down, **Bangkok Burger Co** (BBC; www.bangkokburgercompany.com; Bangla Mall, Soi Bangla; ⏱11am-4am; 📶) is ideal for soaking up the alcohol. You won't miss the Bangla entertainment thanks to its prime position and windows overlooking the mayhem. Gourmet burgers travel the globe from 'Le Parisian' with brie and garlic mushrooms and the 'Aussie' complete with Vegemite mayo to the home-grown 'Bangkok Dangerous' – crispy bacon, Thai green curry sauce and fiery jalapenos. Now you can hit the clubs, but we're not responsible for you from here on!

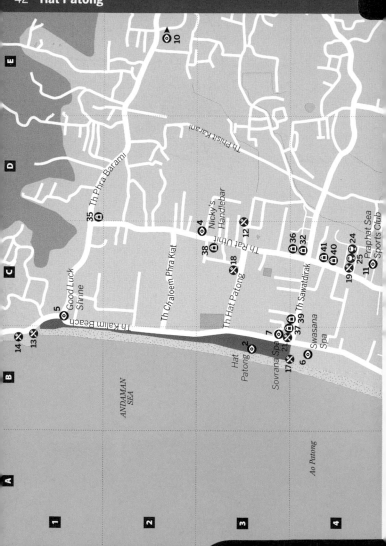

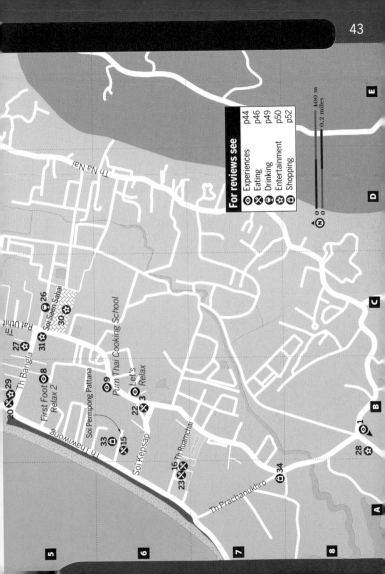

Th Na Nai

Th Rat Uthit

Th Bangla

First Foot
Relax 2

Soi Permpong Pattana

Pum Thai Cooking School

Soi Saen Sabai

Let's
Relax

Soi Kepsap

Th Ruamchai

Th Thawiwong

Th Prachanukhro

20
29
27
8
9
3
22
15
33
16
23
34
28
1
26
30
31

For reviews see

⊙	Experiences	p44
✕	Eating	p46
🍸	Drinking	p49
🎭	Entertainment	p50
🛍	Shopping	p52

N

0   100 m
0   0.2 miles

Experiences

Freedom Beach
BEACH

1 ◎ Map p42, B8

It's just 15 minutes from Patong Beach by long-tail boat, but a whole different world away. If Patong is suffocating you, then you will find freedom on this pristine slice of golden sand where palm trees cast shadows over the clear turquoise waters. (return boat trips 1500B)

Hat Patong
BEACH

2 ◎ Map p42, B3

It may not be a stretch of untouched paradise, but the beach here is action packed with loads of water activities on offer and you don't have to venture far to kick on for the night.

Let's Relax
SPA

3 ◎ Map p42, B6

The cool atrium, gushing with fountains and infused with eucalyptus, is the perfect place to devise your spa strategy. Reflexology then a body scrub? Or would you rather try a Thai herbal steam bath before a hot-stone massage and a facial? Life is full of tough decisions. (✆ 0 7634 6080; www.bloomingspa.com; 209/22-24 Th Rat Uthit; massages/treatments from 300/1200B; ◷ 10.30am-midnight)

Nicky's Handlebar
ADVENTURE SPORTS

4 ◎ Map p42, C3

The custom-made big-beast bikes here are just begging for a spin. They hover around 1500cc, so they're not for amateurs. You'll need a big-bike licence from home, but you won't need a map as Nicky and Kai have been leading Harley tours around Phuket for over a decade. If you want to live out a Ferris Bueller fantasy, take a Ferrari for a lap around Patong (4500B). There's also a bar for post-ride/-drive refreshment (p49) (✆ 0 7633 3211; www.nickyhandlebars.com; 41 Th Rat Uthit; tours incl bike hire per day from 4800B)

Good Luck Shrine
SHRINE

5 ◎ Map p42, C1

A lovely, golden Bodhisattva statue, guarded by carved elephants festooned with flowers, incense and candles, with a sea backdrop. This is a nice spot to connect with the divine or simply make a wish and savour the sound of...silence. (cnr Th Kalim Beach & Th Phra Barami; admission free)

Swasana Spa
SPA

6 ◎ Map p42, B4

This four-star spa is right on the beach at the quiet north end of Patong. The best deal is the traditional Thai massage (850B). You'll be nestled in a cool glass cube on a cushy floor mat with ocean views. (✆ 0 7634 0138; www.impiana.com; 41 Th Thawiwong; treatments from 850B; ◷ 10am-9pm)

Sovrana Spa
SPA

7 ◎ Map p42, B3

Part salon, part shop, this is a popular choice among Patong's spas with

CHRISTER FREDRIKSSON/GETTY IMAGES ©

Freedom Beach

reasonable prices and a host of treatments. Indulge in a massage, facial or both using the in-house Sovrana range of aromatic products, and decide which, or all, you're going to take home. The aloe vera face mask does wonders for those inclined to burn up. Opposite Jung Ceylon. (☏ 0 7634 0265; 198/13 Rat-U-Thit; massages from 300B, package treatments from 1400B; ☺10am-midnight)

First Foot Relax 2 SPA

8 ◎ Map p42, B5

Although pricier than most shop-front massage joints, First Foot Relax 2 is worth it – in fact, it's in a league of its own. There are mosaic washbowls for reflexology clients, the dark-wood interior is infused with lemongrass, and baskets bloom with fresh towels. Splurge and get the seaweed and mud wrap before your massage. (☏ 0 7634 0248; 54/7 Soi Patong Resort; massage from 400B; ☺10am-midnight)

Pum Thai Cooking School COOKING

9 ◎ Map p42, B6

This restaurant chain (with branches in Thailand, the UK and France) holds a range of daily classes catering to those anxious to get back to the beach (45min, 599B) to wannabe master-chefs (6-hour private lesson with Pum herself, 6000B). Some classes include a trip to the market and free cookbooks. Check the website for details and book at least a week in advance. (☎ 0 7634 6269; www.pumthaifoodchain.com; 204/32 Th Rat Uthit)

Jungle Bungy Jump

ADVENTURE SPORTS

10 🎯 Map p42, E2

If you feel like you're getting too relaxed and need a jolt of adrenaline, this 20-storey bungy jump should sort you out. Jumpers have the option to dunk, leap in pairs or experience the Rocket Man, where you'll be shot 50m in the air, then do the bungy on the way down. In business for 20 years, it's built and operated to Kiwi standards. (☎ 0 7632 1351; www.phuketbungy. com; 61/3 Moo 6, Kathu; jump 1600B)

Praphat Sea Sports Club

WATER SPORTS

11 🎯 Map p42, C4

Diving is this club's bread and butter but it also offers deep-sea fishing trips

Top Tip

Hat, Beach...Same, Same.

If your Thai is a little rusty, the most important word you'll probably need to know is Hat. Hat means 'beach' and you'll notice places are referred to as Patong Beach or Hat Patong, Kata Beach and Hat Kata... same, same. And Ko means 'island'. See our Language chapter for more essential holiday Thai.

for those after some black marlin, tuna and barracuda, and it hires boards and offers surfing instruction as well. (☎ 0 7634 4632; www.phuketsea sport.com; 141/11 Soi Royal Paradise; fishing trip for 4 people per day 19,000B, board hire per day 1200B, surf lesson per hr/2hr/4hr 300/1200/2000B)

Eating

The 9th Floor

INTERNATIONAL $$$

12 🍴 Map p42, C3

Brave the dark backstreets, aged facade and dodgy elevator because on the 9th floor it's less NYC ghetto and more swanky Manhattan rooftop... circa the '80s. The fleet of Thai waitresses in snug black minidresses just walked off the set of a Robert Palmer music video, and floor-to-ceiling glass doors slide open inviting sea breezes and a sea of lights. (☎ 0 7634 4311; www.the9thfloor.com; 47 Th Rat Uthit; mains 240-1990B)

Baan Rim Pa

THAI $$$

13 🍴 Map p42, B1

Great Thai food is served with a side order of spectacular views at this institution. Standards are high, with prices to match, but romance is in the air, with candlelight and piano music aplenty. Book ahead and tuck in your shirt. (☎ 0 7634 4079; 223 Th Phra Barami; dishes 215-475B)

White Box INTERNATIONAL $$$

14 Map p42, B1

Housed in, quite literally, a white box, which teeters on the rocky shoreline, this ultramodern minimalist joint is a little bit too cool for school, but they get away with it with these views and tasty gourmet dishes to back it up. (📞 0 7634 6271; www.whiteboxrestaurant. com; 247/5 Th Phra Barami; dishes 320-980B; 🕒 5pm-1am)

The Orchids THAI $

15 Map p42, B6

Get your fantastic, cheap Thai food served in a homely atmosphere. The *larb gai* (minced chicken salad mixed with chilli, mint and coriander; also available with beef or pork) is delicious, plus the Orchids has all the favourite classics you love. Fried ice-cream rounds the meal off nicely. (📞 0 7634 0462; 78/3-4 Soi Permpong Pattana; 50-225B; 🕒 10am-midnight)

Naughty Radish CAFE $$

16 Map p42, A6

Naughty Radish is the nerdy kid who brings carrot sticks to a party. But if Patong's had its partying way with you, thwart your guilt here with some healthy goodness. Create your own salads at this funky cafe, or choose from one of their signature creations. The Japanese Geisha with soft-shell crab, cucumber and wasabi mayo, washed down with a detox juice, is just what the doctor ordered. (www.

Top Tip
Jet Ski Scams

For those planning to hire a jet ski in Phuket, be aware of the risks of one of the island's well-publicised scams, particularly along Patong Beach. There are reports of unscrupulous jet-ski owners who upon your return will claim you've caused damage to the watercraft that was, in fact, pre-existing. Things can turn nasty in their attempts to extort money with reports of physical threats and even police intervention, who are alleged to be involved in the scam. To avoid such unpleasant encounters, insist on inspecting the jet ski prior to use – particularly underneath and along the sides – ideally with the aid of a camera to take photos as proof.

burasari.com; 18/110 Th Ruamchai; signature salads 150-240B; 🕒 11am-9pm; 🖋)

The Beach SEAFOOD $$

17 Map p42, B3

If you can't be arsed changing outta your bathers for lunch, then this is your spot. Plonk down on a plastic chair right on the sand at this aptly named seafood joint. While it's a bit pricier than it should be, the luxury of dining with sand between your toes and the convenience is worth the extra pennies. (Th Kalim Beach; dishes from 180B; 🕒 8am-midnight)

Th Bangla (p41)

Sandwich Shoppe
CAFE $

18 Map p42, C3

You're the master of your meal at this tucked-away cafe. Build your own salads, sandwiches, bagels and breakfasts from an array of options for everything from the bread to the dressing. If you can't decide, there are loads of premade options, from the Whiskey River BBQ chicken foot-long baguette to NY bagels. (www.khunwoody.com; 26-27 Th Aroonsom Plaza; ⏰8am-6pm; 🛜)

Newspaper
THAI $$

19 Map p42, C4

In the heart of Patong's gay-friendly area, this designer boutique inn has a sweet, intimate dining room with woven rope chairs, roses on the tables, muslin-wrapped chandeliers and concrete floors. The menu is typical Thai, and it serves Western breakfasts. (☎0 7634 6275; www.newspaperphuket.com; 125/4-5 Soi Paradise Hotel; ⏰24hr)

Savoey
THAI $$

20 Map p42, B5

On an island packed with weighed-to-order fish grills, this is one of the best. Its huge ice shelf is packed with lobsters, prawns, grouper, red snapper, sole, trevally and barracuda. It has one menu and four dining rooms – two of them on the sand. The food is always great, and the prices are quite reasonable. (☎0 7634 1171; 136 Th Thawiwong; ⏰6.30am-11pm)

Tantra
INDIAN $$

21 Map p42, B3

Better dressed than Phuket's other Indian haunts, Tantra has cushioned floor seating and the sort of creamy North Indian dishes you see back home. (☑08 5909 9929; 186/5 Th Thawiwong; ⏰11am-1am; 🛜)

Yean Korean BBQ
KOREAN $$$

22 Map p42, B6

Bit of a control freak at BBQs? You'll love this place where they leave the grilling up to you. Sizzle up thinly sliced beef, prawns or pork at your table inside or opt for the dimly lit Thai-cushioned floor seating out front. No need to leave your vegetarian friends behind, they'll love the veg stone pot *bimbimbap* (rice topped with crunchy fresh ingredients, egg and fiery chilli paste). (☑0 7634 0955; 210/4 Th Rat Uthit; ⏰noon-midnight)

Ali Baba
INDIAN $$

23 Map p42, A6

Smell that tandoori oven cookin' as you enter this cosy, spotless cafe with its all-year-round tinsel decorations and odd cave-like setting. Serving tasty and traditional Indian, Pakistani and Arabic food cooked by its Indian chef, it counts Patong's Indian residents among its loyal customers. (☑0 7634 9924; 38 Th Ruamchai; ⏰11am-midnight; 🍴)

Sala Bua
FUSION $$$

Enjoy award-winning Asian fusion cuisine in this seaside four-star resort setting. (see 6 ◉ Map p42, B4). Try arugula and baked soft-shell crab and move on to the seared yellow-fin tuna, king scallops or marinated tofu steaks. (☑0 7634 0138; www.impiana.com; 41 Th Thawiwong; ⏰6.30am-10.30pm)

Drinking

Nicky's Handlebar
BAR

It's a fun blast of Easy Rider nostalgia at this biker bar (see 4 ◉ Map p42, C3), which is welcoming to all – wheels or no wheels. But you can get your own wheels by asking about the Harleys for hire at their attached shop (p44). Careful lifting those menus, they weigh a ton, made from hubcaps and heavy disc brakes. If you hired a scooter, maybe park it up the road... (☑0 7634 3211-3; www.nickyhandlebars.com; 41 Th Rat Uthit)

⬤ Local Life
Mae Ubol Market

This **market** (Map p42, D7; Th Na Nai; admission free; ⏰7am-noon & 5pm-4am) has two shifts. In the morning, head to the warehouse, where you'll see a bustling fresh market hard at haggle; it's an entertaining scene. At 5pm the night market opens for business, meaning you can eat good Thai food and fresh seafood all night long.

Understand
Connect Four!

Is it an innocent children's game or a bar girl's ruse to score your cash 100B at a time? You'll find out on Th Bangla. It seems an innocent enough pastime when you belly up to the bar. You'll play a game or two for a few hundred baht while you sip another Singha. But know that your opponent is a Connect Four mastermind. She will win, quickly and easily. You'll go for double or nothing. Your friends will help you strategise. And she'll win again. Even easier this time. Be afraid. Be very afraid.

White Box   BAR

Oozing sex appeal, the rooftop lounge of this ultracool restaurant (see **14** Map p42, B1) is a great spot for a cocktail overlooking Patong Bay. Local DJs spin chill-out tunes most weekends and everyone's got their best model pouts on. (www.whiteboxrestaurant.com; 247/5 Th Phra Barami; ☺5pm-1am)

Backstage   BAR

24 🍺 Map p42, C4

Part of the Paradise Complex gay-friendly block of bars and clubs, gay travellers and locals mingle at this relaxed bar in a casual environment minus the sleaze. Sign up for the men-only BBQ pool party every Saturday where 800B gets you transport, food and an open bar. Owner, Rob, is your sociable host and a wealth of knowledge on all things gay-friendly in Patong. (www.backstage.asia; 127/10-11 Th Rat Uthit, Paradise Complex; ☺1pm-2am; 🛜)

Connect   BAR

25 🍺 Map p42, C4

With its soft lighting and cheap drinks, this is a great place to start the night off in Patong's gay district. It also runs Gay Day tours to a private beach for 1950B with all-inclusive food and drinks. (Th Rat Uthit, Paradise Complex; ☺8pm-2am; 🛜)

The Yorkshire Hotel   PUB

26 🍺 Map p42, C5

Enjoy football games among the English at this sleek sports bar, where flat screens beam clear and the beer is icy. (☎0 7634 0904; www.yorkshireinn.com; 169/16 Soi Saen Sabai; ☺7am-midnight)

Entertainment
Seduction   CLUB

27 ⭐ Map p42, C5

One of Patong's most pumpin' nightclubs comes courtesy of a Finnish club impresario. Known for buying up Helsinki's best clubs, he opened this one in 2006 and has since attracted international party people dancing to well-known global DJs. The design, lighting and sound system are all top shelf. The party doesn't start rocking

till the wee small hours. (www.seduc
tiondisco.com; 39/1 Th Bangla; admission
varies; ⊙10pm-4am)

Phuket Simon Cabaret   CABARET

28 ⭐ Map p42, B8

The 600-seat theatre is grand, the costumes are gorgeous and the ladyboys...
convincing. Welcome to Phuket Simon
Cabaret, the number-one ladyboy
show in town, and quintessential
Patong experience. The house is often
full so book ahead. (☎0 7634 2114-6;
www.phuket-simoncabaret.com; 8 Th Sirirach;
admission normal/VIP seats 700/800B;
⊙performances 6, 7.45 & 9.30pm nightly)

Factory Bar   BAR, CLUB

29 ⭐ Map p42, B5

Hidden up a flight of stairs, next to
the Red Hot Club, is one of Bangla's
newest establishments. Concrete
floors and plush couches style it up,
while pool tables and foosball keep
things casual. There are several nooks
and crannies to hide away in here, but
if you're more the showboatin' type
then the sweaty dancefloor, blast-
ing soundsystem and music vids on
screens provide the perfect tools. (www.
factorybarphuket.com; 1-4/198 Th Bangla;
⊙7pm-1am)

CHRISTER FREDRIKSSON/GETTY IMAGES ©

Phuket Simon Cabaret

Sound Phuket

NIGHTCLUB

30 Map p42, C5

When internationally renowned DJs come to Phuket these days, they are usually gigging amid the rounded, futuristic environs of Sound, Patong's hottest (and least sleazy) nightclub. If top-shelf DJs are on the decks, expect to pay up to 300B for entry. (☏0 7636 6163; www.soundphuket.com; 193 Th Rat Uthit, Jung Ceylon, Unit 2303; admission varies; ☺10pm-4am)

Bangla Boxing Stadium

THAI BOXING

31 Map p42, C5

Old name, new stadium, same game: a packed line-up of competitive *moo•ay tai* (Thai boxing; also *muay thai*) bouts. (☏0 7282 2348; Th Phisit Karani; admission 1000-1500B; ☺9-11.30pm Tue, Wed, Fri & Sun)

Shopping

Amarit

HANDICRAFTS

32 Map p42, C4

Small but lovely art and antique shop stocked with Thai paintings and Buddha sculptures. It's definitely worth a look if you are contemplating converting your garden back home to Buddhism. (☏08 1892 9044; 99/2 Th Rat Uthit; ☺2-11pm Mon-Sat)

Baan Thai Antiques

ANTIQUES

33 Map p42, B6

A glorious collection of antiques and new-production traditional art from Myanmar (Burma), China, Laos and Thailand crowd this small shop. There are 70-year-old alabaster Buddhas, gongs, temple bells (the real thing), lacquerware, ceramics and teak-wood reliefs. Some are reasonably priced while the majority are more for serious collectors. Shipping can be arranged. (☏0 7629 2274; www.baanthai -antique.com; 80/5 Soi Permpong Pattana; ☺10am-11pm)

Baanboonpitak

HANDICRAFTS

34 Map p42, A7

Ready for a treasure hunt? Hidden in this dusty antique shop is an array of teak sculpture, paintings, some excellent bronze work, massive buffalo-skin drums, bejewelled royal dogs and a lot of high-quality teak furniture. So get dirty and find something beautiful. The sardonically sweet shopkeeper will arrange shipping. (☏0 7634 1789; 30 Th Prachanukhro; ☺10am-7pm)

Art Galleries

ART

35 Map p42, D1

At the end of the T-intersection of Th Rat Uthit and Th Phra Barami sits this cluster of small art galleries, worth having a look at if you're in the market for some original local art. The

Understand
Sex Tourism

While Thailand has a long and complex relationship with prostitution, today it's an industry that's targeted to foreign tourists – a legacy left behind from the Vietnam War days. It's very visible in Phuket, particularly in Patong.

Due to international pressure from the UN, prostitution was declared illegal in 1960, yet laws against prostitution are often ambiguous and unenforced. Furthermore, the unintended consequence of prostitution prohibitions is the lawless working environment it creates for women who enter the industry. Sex work becomes the domain of criminal networks that are often involved in other illicit activities and circumvent the laws through bribes and violence. Sex workers are not afforded the rights of other workers: there is no minimum wage; no required vacation, sick leave or break time; no deductions for social security or employee-sponsored health insurance and no legal redress. Bars can set their own punitive rules that fine a worker if she doesn't smile enough, arrives late or doesn't meet the drink quota. EMPOWER reported that many sex workers will owe money to the bar at the end of the month through these deductions. In effect, these women have to pay to be prostitutes.

Child Prostitution
According to ECPAT (End Child Prostitution & Trafficking), there are currently 30,000 to 40,000 children involved in prostitution in Thailand, though estimates are unreliable. According to Chulalongkorn University, the number of children may be as as high as 800,000. In 1996 Thailand passed a reform law to address the issue of child prostitution (defined into two tiers: 15 to 18 years old and under 15). Fines and jail time are assigned to customers, establishment owners and even parents involved in child prostitution (under the old law only prostitutes were culpable). Many countries also have extraterritorial legislation that allows nationals to be prosecuted in their own country for such crimes committed in Thailand. Responsible travellers can help to stop child-sex tourism by reporting suspicious behaviour on a dedicated hotline (☏1300) or reporting the individual directly to the embassy of the offender's nationality.

Nop Art with its bright, bold artworks of Thai scenes (floating markets, sailboats on the sea and coconut drinks), and Art Heart Gallery's vibrant abstract pieces, are the standouts. (☎08 9197 6778; cnr Th Rat Uthit & Th Phra Barami; ☺9am-9pm)

Sainamyen Plaza   MARKET

36 🔒 Map p42, C4

This undercover market is a one-stop shop for souvenirs, clothing, luggage, socks, bikinis and more. (Th Rat Uthit; ☺10am-10pm)

Baru   CLOTHING

37 🔒 Map p42, B3

Packed in a hurry and got those old, faded, baggy-bum bikinis on all holiday? Throw them out and pack yourself in tight with some of the hot, skimpy and well-priced bikinis (900B to 3000B) on offer at Baru. Light wraps and dresses in subtle tribal design leave a little more to the imagination and make dressing up for dinner easy. (☎0 7634 6425; www.barufashion.com; 12 Th Sawatdirak; ☺9.30am-11pm)

Jung Ceylon   MALL

The major chain stores (Apple, Starbucks, The Body Shop, Adidas) are here at Jung Ceylon (see **30** ⭐ Map p42, C5), along with many surf shops and plush cinemas, and the Sino-Phuket wing has a decent international restaurant row. Gun lovers, if you feel like letting off a round after lunch, head to the laser shooting gallery on the top floor, of course. (Th Rat Uthit; ☺11am-10pm)

Understand
Gay Pride in Phuket

Although there are big gay pride celebrations in Bangkok and Pattaya, the Phuket Gay Pride Festival is considered by many to be the best in Thailand. The date has changed several times, but it usually lands between February and April. Whenever it blooms, the whole island – but the town of Patong specifically – is packed with (mostly male) revellers from all over the world. The main events of the four-day weekend party are a huge beach-volleyball tournament and, of course, the Grand Parade, featuring floats, cheering crowds and beautiful costumes in the streets of Patong. In recent years, the festival has also included social-responsibility campaigns against child prostitution and substance abuse, and for HIV awareness. Any other time of year, the backstreets off Th Rat Uthit in Patong (Paradise Complex) is where you'll find Phuket's gay pulse. For more information about the scene, go to www.gaypatong.com.

Bookshop

BOOKSTORE

38 Map p42, C3

A secondhand stall selling books in many languages including German, Scandinavian, English and Japanese. (Th Rat Uthit; books from 180B; ⏱10am-10pm)

Silverberry

JEWELLERY

39 Map p42, C4

Need some holiday bling? Silverberry has a great choice of sterling silver and gold pendants, rings, necklaces and whatever else you can drape off you, all handmade by Thai and Balinese silversmiths. (www.silverberry.com; 1/10 Th Sawadirak; ⏱10am-10pm)

Metal Art

ART

40 Map p42, C4

Sci-fi robotic sculptures made entirely from scrap-metal car parts crowd this quirky art shop. You've got everything from the Terminator and Boba Fett to Ned Kelly. Even if you're not a nerd, it's still worth popping in to admire the handiwork. (📞0 7629 6453; That Siam, Thailand Plaza; ⏱10am-10pm)

PAUL BROWN/ALAMY ©

Jung Ceylon

J&L Motorbike Shop

ART

41 Map p42, C4

It looks like an ordinary garage, but inside are some amazing demonic dinosaur sculptures crafted from old motorcycle parts. A must see for all 10 year olds. (106 Th Rat Uthit; admission free; ⏱9am-9pm)

Explore

Hat Karon & Hat Kata

Showcasing all that's great about Phuket, the conjoined twin beach towns of Kata and Karon are rightfully popular choices. Kata is an energetic blend of bohemia and ritz, while Karon is the restrained older sibling. Their long beaches, great eateries and bars – minus the excesses of Patong – reel in families and backpackers, along with a brigade of Scandinavian and Russian tourists.

ANDREAS ROSE/GETTY IMAGES ©

The Region in a Day

☀ After breakfast, make the journey to **Big Buddha** (p58) before the heat kicks in, then opt for beachside luxury at **Re Ká Ta** (p63) beach club, or rent a deckchair to laze on the sand. Grab lunch at **Mom Tri's Kitchen** (p65) and appreciate the fantastic beach views.

☀ From here you can take your pick from a lazy afternoon of a beach siesta, a round of minigolf at **Dino Park** (p64) with the kids or an elephant trek at **Kok Chang Safari** (p63). Otherwise, take a break from the heat and go underwater on a dive at **Hat Kata Yai** (p62) or **Hat Karon** (p62; pictured left).

☽ Hike up to **After Beach Bar** (p68) for the sublime sunset with panoramic views and grab a beer and *pàt tai* while you're here, or otherwise splurge at the fancy **Boathouse** (p65) before heading to **Ska Bar** (p69) or **Rick 'n' Roll Music Cafe** (p69) to drink the night away.

◉ Top Experiences
Big Buddha (p58)

♥ Best of Kata & Karon
Dining
Boathouse Wine & Grill (p65)

Capannina (p65)

Bella Vista (p65)

Drinking
After Beach Bar & Restaurant (p68)

On the Rocks (p69)

Ska Bar (p69)

Rick 'n' Roll Music Cafe (p69)

Getting There

🚕 **Taxi** A taxi from the airport costs around 750B; from Phuket Town and Patong 600B.

Minibus Minibus from the airport (min 11 people) costs 180B.

Sŏrngtăaou These run to both Kata and Karon from Phuket Town (per person 30B).

Top Experiences
Big Buddha

Set high on the top of the Nakkerd hills, north-west of Chalong circle and visible from almost half of the island, the Big Buddha definitely has an energetic pulse and some of the best views of Phuket. It might feel more tourist-trap than spiritual but the sheer size and the surrounds is reason enough to linger a while.

👁 Off Map p60

mingmongkolphuket.com

off Hwy 402, north of Chalong Circle

admission free

Don't Miss

The Buddha
Over the last 20 years construction on Phuket hasn't stopped, so it means something when locals refer to the Big Buddha as Phuket's most important development in the last 100 years. Overseen by a local developer-turned-devout-Buddhist, more than 60 labourers and crafts-people have almost completed one of the largest Buddha statues on earth.

The Views
From the Buddha's plateau you can peer into Kata's perfect turquoise bay and glimpse the shimmering Karon strand. And while you take in the view, the serenity amid the tinkling bells and the yellow Buddhist flags flapping in the wind to a background of soft dharma music may just have you sensing something divine.

Meditation
You're on holiday so you probably won't be spending hours meditating, but you're in luck. Just before you enter, you'll find the seven-minute happiness meditation – free meditation in the morning from 8am, every day.

CHARLES HOWELL/ALAMY ©

☑ Top Tips

▶ Túk-túk or taxi from Kata or Karon is around 600B.

▶ If you're driving yourself, it's about 6km to the top from the main road. Drive with care as accidents are common.

▶ As with all religious sites, dress conserva-tively. For women, skirts need to be past the knee and shoulders should be covered up. You'll be given a shawl to wear at the gate if needed.

✕ Take a Break

There are several ven-dors selling drinks and snacks and the open-air **Nakkerd Seaview** restaurant has some decent food and, of course, excellent views.

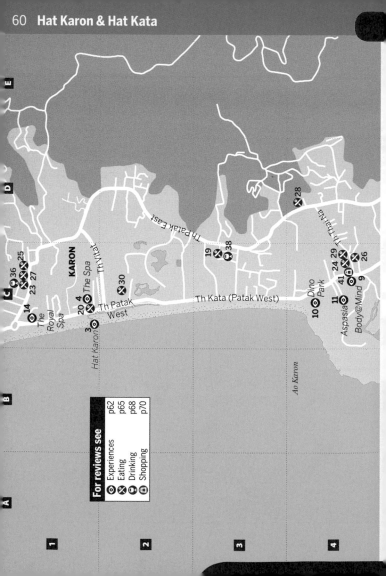

KARON

The Royal Spa

The Spa

Th Vital

Th Patak East

Th Patak West

Th Kata (Patak West)

Hat Karon

Th Thalang

Ao Karon

Dino Park

Aspasia

Body@Mind

36
25
23 27
14
20 4
30
3
19 38
28
24 29
41 9
26
10
11

Experiences

Boathouse Cooking Class

COOKING

1 Map p60, D6

One of Phuket's most acclaimed restaurants gives away some of their secrets at these fantastic weekend cooking classes with their renowned chef, Rattana. You'll learn how to make five authentic Thai dishes but will get to taste nine. The price includes lunch, free transport and a recipe book (so you don't forget when hosting those dinner parties back home). (☎ 0 7633 0015-7; www.boathousephuket.com/cooking_classes; 182 Koktanode Rd, Kata; 1/2 days 2200/3500B; ⊙10am-2pm Sat & Sun)

Hat Kata Yai

BEACH

2 Map p60, C5

Kata Beach is split into two areas: Kata Yai (known as the main Kata beach) and Kata Noi (which curves around the bay). Both are stunning and retain their bohemian feel despite some upmarket dining and resorts. Main outfitters are Dive Asia and Sunrise Divers (see p136).

Hat Karon

BEACH

3 Map p60, C1

This long stretch of squeaky sand is popular with families, and while it does get busy, there are always plenty of spots to spread out. Dive Asia and Sunrise Divers can arrange trips.

INGOLF POMPE/GETTY IMAGES ©

View across Hat Kata Yai and Hat Karon

The Spa

SPA

4 ⊙ Map p60, C1

You won't know yourself after this. Your mind will be revitalised, your body wrapped in mud, your skin scrubbed with dead sea salts before you're dunked into an aromatic floral milk bath. Located within the expansive grounds of the Mövenpick, this is one of the most atmospheric spas in Karon, with rooms leading off a tree-filled tropical garden. Get romantic with 2½ hour massages for couples (6700B). (☑0 7639 6139; www.moevenpick -hotels.com/en/asia/thailand/phuket/resort -phuket-karon-beach; 509 Patak Rd, Karon; 1hr massage from 1700B; ⊙9am-9pm)

Kok Chang Safari

ANIMAL INTERACTION

5 ⊙ Map p60, E8

This well-run elephant camp is easily one of the best in Phuket (the animals here are healthy). Longer trips have magical seaviews from the top of the mountain and kids aged four to 11 enter half price. If you're not keen on riding an elephant, you can still pop in to feed them a banana, for a donation. (☑08 9591 9413; www.kokchangsafari.com; 287 Moo 2, Hwy 4233, Kata; elephant safari 20/30/50 mins 600/800/1000B; ⊙8.30am-5.30pm)

Karon View Point

VIEWPOINT

6 ⊙ Map p60, D8

Further along the highway from After Beach Bar (p68) is this majestic sunset viewpoint. From here, your view extends from the northern reaches of Karon to the Laem Phromthep. Don't linger late at night as there have been attacks and robberies in the wee hours. (Hwy 4233, Kata)

Re Ká Ta

BEACH CLUB

7 ⊙ Map p60, C6

Of the chic beach clubs that have sprung up in Phuket, Re Ká Ta is the chicest. It's run by the guys from the Boathouse. Entry here gets a day of luxury among the beautiful people, lounging in soft faux-leather beds, deckchairs and hammocks, or sipping cocktails in the freshwater infinity pool. Better yet, the entry fee includes credit at the restaurant and bar. Thursday is ladies' night, which means a free cocktail and manicure. (☑0 7633 0421; www.rekataphuket.com; 182 Koktanode Rd, Kata; entry low/high season 500/1000B incl food & drinks; ⊙9am-midnight)

Spa Royale

SPA

8 ⊙ Map p60, C7

Organic spa products, seaside treatment rooms with private steam baths and highly skilled therapists make this one of the top spas in southern Phuket. Its 90-minute aromatherapy massage is hard to beat. (☑0 7633 3568; www.villaroyalephuket.com; 12 Th Kata Noi, Kata; treatments from 1200B; ⊙9am-8pm)

Body@Mind

SPA

9 ⊙ Map p60, C4

A nice 'tweener. It's more upscale than the shopfront spas and not as pricey as the resort spas. It has a full menu of massages, wraps, scrubs and half-day packages, and it provides a free round-trip transfer from your hotel. (☑0 7639 8274; www.body-mindspa.com; 558/7-12 Th Patak West, Kata; massages/spa packages from 600/1200B; ☉9am-10pm)

Dino Park   AMUSEMENT PARK

10 ◉ Map p60, C4

Jurassic Park meets minigolf at this bizarre park on the southern edge of Hat Karon. It's a maze of caves, lagoons, leafy gardens, dinosaur statues and even a prehistoric turd, all spread over 18 holes of putting greens. Kids and adults will dig it equally. (☑0 7639 8274; www.dinopark.com; Th Patak West, Karon; adult/child 240/180B; ☉10am-midnight)

Local Life
Wat Karon

Set back from the road is a relatively new temple complex, **Wat Karon** (Map p60 C1; Th Patak East; admission free), with a small shrine occupied by a seated, black-stone Buddha. Behind it is the striking tiered-roof crematorium, which only opens on ceremonial days. The grounds are lush with banana, palm and mango trees. Arguably, however, the main reason to visit is for its Tuesday and Saturday night market (from 5pm), which has stalls selling clothes, accessories and food.

Aspasia   SPA

11 ◉ Map p60, C4

A good day-spa option is hidden away at a seaside condo resort on the headland between Kata and Karon. The interior is cosy and very Zen with sliding rice-paper doors dividing the treatment rooms. Try the red sweet body scrub, a mixture of sesame, honey and fresh orange juice. It's a sweaty and steep hike from the main road, so a túk-túk isn't a bad option. (☑0 7628 4430; www.aspasiaphuket.com; 1/3 Th Laem Sai, Kata; treatments from 1000B; ☉10am-8pm)

Kata Hot Yoga   YOGA

12 ◉ Map p60, D6

Crave more heat? Consider a class at Kata Hot Yoga. Class times vary according to the season but usually run a few times per weekday and on weekend evenings. Check the website for details. (☑0 7660 5950; www.katahotyoga.com; 217 Th Khoktanod, Kata; per class 500B)

Phuket Surf   SURFING

13 ◉ Map p60, C6

Located at Phuket's most well known surf spot on the southern cove of Hat Kata Yai, Phuket Surf offers half-day lessons and board rentals. Check its website for more info about local surf breaks. (☑08 7934 6654, 08 7889 7308; www.phuketsurf.com; Th Koktanod, Kata; lessons 1500B; board rental per hr/day 150/500B; ☉Apr–late-Oct)

The Royal Spa
SPA

14 Map p60, C1

Part of the Sea Sands Resort, this four-star spa delivers both luxury and therapy. It has a nice selection of Thai treatments, but also offers Ayurvedic and hot-stone massage. (0 7628 6464; 206 Th Karon, Karon; treatments from 1850B; ⏰10am-7pm)

Longtail Charters
BOATING

15 Map p60, D6

Full- and half-day charters are available to Coral island and Ko Bon from Hat Kata. (Southern end of Hat Kata Yai; from 2000B)

Eating

Boathouse
Wine & Grill
FRENCH, THAI **$$$**

With French cuisine, candlelit tables, red roses and a sublime beachfront setting at the southern end of Hat Kata, the Boathouse (see **1** Map p60, D6) is still the best place for a romantic dinner or special occasion. While the food can be hit and miss, the atmosphere and the long wine list are spot on. It's a fancy place, so sunburned dudes in tank tops tend to be a little conspicuous. Book ahead to secure a table close to the sand. (0 7633 0015; www.boathousephuket.com; 182 Koktanod Rd, Kata; mains from 350B; ⏰6.30am-11pm)

Capannina
ITALIAN **$$**

16 Map p60, D5

Everything here – from the pasta to the sauces – is made fresh, and you can taste it. While service can be inconsistent, the ravioli and gnocchi are reliably fantastic, the risotto comes highly recommended, and the pizzas, *bellisimo*. It gets crowded during the high season, so you may want to reserve ahead. (0 7628 4318; www. capannina-phuket.com; 30/9 Moo 2, Th Kata, Kata; mains 200-700B)

Bella Vista
EUROPEAN, THAI **$$**

17 Map p60, C6

Perched above Ska Bar at the southern end of Hat Kata, this Swiss-run restaurant shares the same beautiful banyan tree and stunning sea views. Go for the well-priced mussel cream soup for lunch, swirling with shellfish and served with bread. The seafood basket is pricey but comes with massive servings of two rock lobsters, two Phuket lobsters, giant tiger prawns, crab, the works. And did we mention the view? (Villa Elisabeth Guesthouse, 2/29 Th Patak, Kata; main 120-500B)

Mom Tri's
Kitchen
MEDITERRANEAN **$$$**

18 Map p60, C7

Another 'special occasion' choice or simply a good spot for an intimate and upmarket lunch, Mom Tri's Kitchen offers fusion haute cuisine and fine wines, while diners overlook breathtaking Hat Kata Noi. (📞 0 7633 3568; Th Kata Noi, Kata; mains 590-1850B; ⏰6.30am-11.30pm)

Mama Noi's

THAI, ITALIAN $

19 Map p60, C3

Repeat visitors adore this place, which churns out fantastic Thai and Italian pasta dishes and has a good local vibe. It does a superb *gaeng som* (southern Thai curry with fish and prawns), it bakes its own baguettes every morning and it has the best banana shake on the island. (📞0 7628 6272; 291/1-2 Moo 3, Th Patak East, Karon Plaza; dishes 80-190B; ⏰7.30am-10pm)

Sandbar Restaurant

PIZZA $$

20 ✘ Map p60, C1

It may be across the road from the beach, but this is the only place you can dine in Karon with the sand between your toes. Flaming bamboo torches and primitive wooden rope-bound love seats create a Survivor-like ambience, and the pizzas are pretty tasty, too. Two-for-one happy hour is from 5pm to 7pm and 11pm to midnight. (509 Th Kata (Patak West); pizzas from 350B; ⏰5pm-1am)

Ratri

ITALIAN, BAR $$

21 ✘ Map p60, D5

Your calves will burn after this 90-degree climb up Kata Hill, but it's well worth it for the authentic Italian food, suave decor and ocean views. Many dishes include Italian imported ingredients, such as the porcini and

black-truffle risotto, and pastas are homemade. Dine on the patio or indoors with live jazz. If you book ahead, there's a pick-up service for the area. (📞0 7633 3538; 74/1 Patak Rd, Kata; mains 180-850B; ⏰5pm-midnight)

Two Chefs

INTERNATIONAL $$

22 ✘ Map p60, D6

Two Chefs is slowly taking over Kata and Karon, but this original location is still the most popular. It's your classic bar and grill with plenty of comfort food minus the spice for a night. Get stuck into herb grilled chicken breasts, blackened salmon burgers or tender grilled rib eye and chips washed down with a cold frothy. (📞0 7628 4155; www.twochefs.com; 229 Koktanod (Patak West), Kata; 175-795B; ⏰lunch & dinner; 📶)

Great Food of India

INDIAN $$

23 ✘ Map p60, C1

They're not lying. The wide range of curries at this family-owned cafe is fantastic. It also does tasty kebabs, tandoori chicken and fish tikka. Takeaway and free home delivery is available in the Karon area. (📞08 1676 7512; 514/11 Th Patak, Karon; mains 290-500B; ⏰11am-11pm; 📶)

Kampong Kata Hill

THAI $$

24 ✘ Map p60, C4

A great option for those in search of not only some decent Thai food, but the experience of dining in a traditional Ahyuttaya teakwood pavilion

DAVID AUSTIN/ALAMY ©

Crispy duck and mango spring rolls at Boathouse Wine & Grill (p65)

chock-a-block with weathered Thai antiques and Buddhist motifs. Sure, it's a bit touristy, yet it's undeniably atmospheric. There are two pavilions, one with great views of Kata, the other with more-contemporary outdoor seating. (📞0 7633 0103; Th Patak West, Kata; 190-350B; ⊙noon-10pm; 🍴)

Red Onion
THAI $

25 🍽 Map p60, C1

Inexplicably busy, this no-frills open-air Thai restaurant sure knows how to draw a crowd. In fact it's not unusual to see people queuing to get in. The food is decent, but not worth queuing for, and neither is the service, so perhaps it's the cheap prices and generous portions that draws people

here. The mixed grilled seafood platters are a good pick, as is the crispy duck. (Th Patak East, Karon; 90-350B; ⊙2-10.30pm; 🍴)

Kwong Shop Seafood
THAI SEAFOOD $

26 🍽 Map p60, C4

Using enticing displays of fresh seafood as bait, this old-school Thai favourite has been reeling in hungry customers for more than 25 years now. It's cheap and cheerful, and its walls are a visual feast of coins, notes and grandfather clocks. Beer is cheap, too. (66 Th Thai Na, Kata; mains 100-300B; ⊙8.30am-midnight; 🍴)

Karon Seafood
THAI **$$**

27 Map p60, C1

This place is definitely not off the beaten track, but sometimes that's OK. Hordes descend for delicacies such as sliced fish in green curry, and squid with basil and chilli. It also has a menu with 10 vegetarian items. (☑0 7639 6797; 514 Moo 1, Th Patak East, Karon; ⏰11am-11pm)

Pad Thai Shop
THAI **$**

28 Map p60, D4

A great option for those who like to keep it local, this no-frills open-air shed does authentic *pàt tai* wrapped in a fresh banana leaf. It's located on the busy main road behind Karon,

---

Understand
Rip Tides

Rip tides are the number one danger for tourists visiting Phuket's beaches. During the May to October monsoon, large waves and fierce undertows sometimes make it too dangerous to swim. Dozens of drownings occur every year on Phuket's beaches, especially on Laem Singh, Kamala and Karon. Red flags are posted to warn bathers of serious rip tides. In our time spent on Karon beach we witnessed no less than five people rescued in a few hours – lesson being: don't swim in the red-flagged areas!

---

just north of the tacky Ping Pong bar. (Th Patak East, Karon; dishes from 60B; ⏰8am-7pm)

Siam Thai Food
THAI **$**

29 Map p60, C4

Cute little Thai cafe–restaurant with an open-air terrace decorated with pot plants and flowers, and a homely interior that doubles as the friendly owner's loungeroom. There's a wide selection of Thai food to choose from, including decent vegetarian options. (Th Thai Na, Karon; mains 120-450B; ⏰8am-10pm)

Bai Toey
THAI **$$**

30 Map p60, C2

A charming Thai bistro with shaded outdoor patio and indoor seating. It has the traditional curry, stir-fry and noodle dishes, but you'd do well to sample its Thai-style grilled beef. (☑08 1691 6202; Soi Old Phuket; meals 200-250B)

Drinking

After Beach Bar & Restaurant
BAR

31 Map p60, D7

It's a sweaty climb (or a 200B túk-túk ride), but once you're here, you'll go crazy over how glorious the view is from this stilted thatched bar hanging off a cliff above Kata. Rocky peninsulas, 180-degree sea views and palm-dappled hills set to a soundtrack of

Bob Marley make it the perfect place for Phuket's sunsets. When the fireball finally drops, the lights of fishing boats blanket the horizon. It also does some of the best *pàt tai* on the island. Yep, life up here is pretty good. (☏08 1894 3750; Hwy 4233, Kata; ⏰9am-midnight)

On the Rocks
BAR

32 🚇 Map p60, C8

On a picturesque cove dominated by a string of ritzy resorts, at the end of the beach lies one of our favourite hideaway bars on Phuket. Its Gilligan's Island set-up is blissfully simple, with a few ramshackle tables and chairs plonked in the sand, a shady bar under the trees, and not a worry in the world. (Hat Kata Noi)

Ska Bar
BAR

At Kata's southernmost cove, tucked into the rocks and seemingly intertwined with the trunk of a grand old banyan tree, Ska (see **17** 🍴 Map p60, C6) is our choice for oceanside sundowners. The Thai bartenders add to the funky Rasta vibe, and the canopy dangles with buoys, paper lanterns and flags of the world. (186/12 Th Koktanod, Kata; ⏰till late)

Rick 'n' Roll Music Cafe
BAR

33 🚇 Map p60, C5

The only genuine backpacker hangout in Phuket, friendly American owner Rick knows how to show punters a good time. The intimate bamboo bar is a great spot to meet other travellers,

and things usually kick on from here. Live music is often on the cards, and there are also barbecues, pub crawls, local tours and dive trips to be booked – PADI-certificate divers get a 15% discount from the bar. (www.rnrhostel.com; 100/51 Th Kata, Kata; ⏰7am-late; 🛜)

Mr Pan's Mini Art Space
BAR

34 🚇 Map p60, D5

Hands down the quirkiest bar in Phuket, Mr Pan's is a psychadelic multi-use cramped space stacked with uniquely brushed canvasses celebrating the feminine form. Live music is held regularly and there's an attached tattoo parlour run by his wife. (☏08 9810 0266; Th Ked Kwan, Kata; ⏰noon-late)

Australia Bar & Grill
BAR

35 🚇 Map p60, C5

With three satellite TVs broadcasting sports from around the world, this is a great place to catch the footy and cricket on the big screen with a meat pie and a cold VB. It's also popular for soccer and motor racing. (www.australiabargrill.com; 100/12-13 Th Kata, Kata Night Plaza, Kata; ⏰4pm-late; 🛜)

Angus O'Tooles
PUB

36 🚇 Map p60, C1

Open '10am till drunk', this authentic dark, wooden Irish pub shows all the big premier league, Aussie Rules, rugby and cricket games on its flat screen and has Guinness and Kilkenny on tap. Also serves up traditional fare of bangers and mash, chip butties and big greasy breakfast cook-ups to cure your hangover – though you may want to skip the black pudding, unless that's your thing. (☎ 0 7639 8262; www.otools-phuket.com; 516/20 Th Patak, Soi Islandia, Karon; ☼ 10am-late; ☎)

The Tube   BAR
37 🍺 Map p60, E6

Run by the guys from Phuket Surf, this laid-back roadside shack is a great hangout to talk about those barrels you got earlier in the day. There's a table made from a longboard, surf videos and a cheap barbecue buffet in the high season. (☎ 08 7889 7308; 157 Th Koktanod (Patak West), Kata; ☼ 7pm-late; ☎)

Nakannoi   BAR
38 🍺 Map p60, G3

A boho art-house hideaway with original canvasses on the walls, found-art decor (including antique motorcycles and bicycles), a concrete island bar and a permanent bandstand, where the owner jams with his mates almost every night after 8pm. (☎ 08 7898 5450; Karon Plaza, Karon; ☼ 5pm-1am)

Danny's Bar 44   BAR
39 🍺 Map p60, D6

One of several bars down this boozy side street, with rows of wooden tables, Connect 4 and a booming PA playing AC/DC. It's like a less seedy version of Patong. (Soi Malisa, Kata; ☼ 3pm-late)

Italian Job   CAFE
40 ☕ Map p60, D6

An Italian coffee lounge with wi-fi, decent pastries, delicious espresso and a loyal morning following. Also does *limoncello* (Italian lemon liqueur) and grappa. (179/1 Th Koktanod, Kata; latte 75B; ☼ 9am-11pm; ☎)

Shopping

Parin Waris   BEAUTY PRODUCTS
41 🛍 Map p60, C4

Homemade organic beauty products such as honey and turmeric shower gel, kaffir lime hair conditioner and coconut soaps on a rope will all keep you clean and smelling like roses...or kaffir lime, turmeric and honey. (12 Th Karon, Karon)

Kata Bookshop   BOOKSTORE
42 🛍 Map p60, D5

It may be one of the world's most famous beach destinations, but it's surprisingly hard to find a good book in Phuket. So thankfully Kata Bookshop has it covered with an excellent stock of secondhand paperbacks in languages from English to Norwegian to Russian – and everything in between. Also has a small selection of postcards. (☎ 0 7633 0109; 35/37 Th Ked Kwan, Kata; ☼ 10am-10pm)

Dino Park (p64)

Elephant Plus

JEWELLERY

43 Map p60, D6

Almost too upscale and tasteful for the Kata crush, here you'll find high-end designer jewellery imagined by Mrs Mom Tri, as well as speciality stemware, antique carvings and top-shelf silk sarongs. (📞0 7633 3423; 184 Th Koktanod, Kata; ⏰noon-5pm & 6-9pm)

Siam Handicrafts

CLOTHING

This place (see **41** Map p60, C4) has linen clothes handmade from hemp and organic cotton, as well as bags and a lovely collection of silver and beaded jewellery, all from northern Thailand. (📞0 7633 3072; pangprasertgul@yahoo.com; 12 Th Karon, Karon; ⏰10am-11pm)

LONELY PLANET/GETTY IMAGES ©

Explore

Rawai

Phuket's original tourist-beach destination, Rawai is now more a working fisherman's beach meets middle-aged-expat enclave. While at first glance it's not an ideal place for a splash, there are some hidden beauties to discover around here. It's worth a visit for the laid-back vibe, seafood grills and lush coastal hills that tumble into the Andaman Sea forming Laem Phromthep, Phuket's southernmost point.

The Region in a Day

It's all about kicking back when in Rawai, so start off late with a pastry at the **German bakery** (p81) before wandering around **Wat Chalong** (p79) to take in the spiritual atmosphere. Then head straight to **Hat Ya Nui** (p77) for a little slice of pristine beach with a backdrop of mountains, minus the crowds.

Take the afternoon to check out some of the vibrant art at **Phuket Art Village** (p78) or head out on a horse ride along the beach with **Phuket Riding Club** (p79). In the late afternoon, you'll want to start making your way to **Laem Phromthep** (p74), arguably the island's best viewpoint, to take in that sensational sunset.

Once the sun goes down, ease into balmy laid-back nights in Rawai. Gorge on seafood at one of the **beachfront grills** (p80) or dine on NZ lamb shanks under the thatched roof at **Rum Jungle** (p79). While away the night with cocktails at **Nikita's** (p82; pictured left), on the rocky waterfront, to the sounds of long-tail boats bobbing in the sea.

👁 Top Experiences
Laem Phromthep (p74)

❤ Best of Rawai
Dining
Rum Jungle (p79)

Baan Rimlay (p80)

Da Vinci (p80)

Drinking
Royal Phuket Yacht Club (p82)

Nikita's (p82)

Getting There

Sŏrngtăaou These run from Phuket Town's fountain circle at Th Ranong (30B) – some continue on to Hat Nai Han, but not all of them so ask first.

🚕 Taxi Private taxi to Rawai and Hat Nai Han from the airport costs 700B; to Patong or Phuket Town costs 500B.

Top Experiences
Laem Phromthep

If you want to see the luscious Andaman Sea bend around Phuket, then you come here, to the island's southernmost point. You won't be alone, but once you scan the 270 degrees of Andaman Sea, noticing how elegantly it arcs around the cape below where local fishermen cast into the waves from the jutting rocks, you'll forget everyone around you.

 Map p76, B4

Hwy 4233

admission free

Elephant shrine

Don't Miss

The Views

There's a reason why busloads of tourists and hordes of Thai locals descend on Laem Phromthep every afternoon. From the viewpoint there are panoramic vistas from the southern tip of the island all the way to Nai Han Beach, across the azure tropical waters of the island-dotted Andaman Sea. But the sunset is the real reason to visit. People lie on the grass or perch on the palm-tree lined concrete wall to bask in the final moments of the warm sun before it drops into the sea.

Lighthouse

The lighthouse was built in 1996 to commemorate the Golden Jubilee of HM King Bhumibol Adulyadej. At the very top, you will gain an elevated view of the sunset and will likely have better photo opportunities away from the majority of people. There's a sunset board out the front of the lighthouse telling you the time of the sunrise and sunset for the day.

Elephant Shrine

Also on the top of the hill is a small, evocative elephant shrine surrounded by hundreds of small elephant statues, which represent wisdom and strength in the Buddhist teaching, and where locals pray.

☑ Top Tips

▶ At sunset the hordes descend in luxury buses, so if you crave privacy, take the faint fishermen's trail downhill to the rocky peninsula that reaches into the ocean and watch the sun drop in peace.

▶ If you want to avoid the crowds altogether, then arrive around 4pm or 5pm. You'll get to appreciate the views in more solitude, grab a drink then head back for the sunset.

▶ Do not forget your camera.

▶ Note there is no smoking and no alcohol allowed at the viewpoint.

✖ Take a Break

Laem Phromthep Cape restaurant is a lovely spot for a drink and a snack, with tables on the grass and sea views.

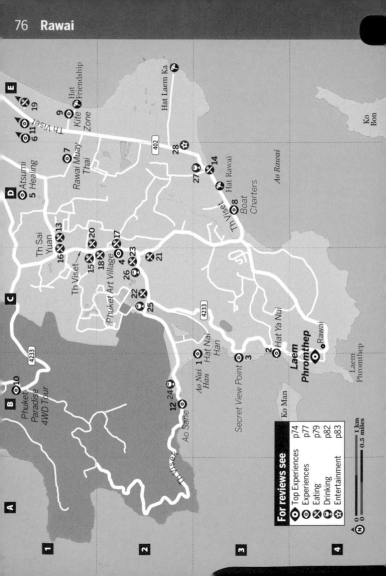

Hat Laem Ka

Ko
Bon

Hat Friendship

Kite
Zone

19

Th Viset

11
6

9

7
Rawai Muay
Thai

402

28

27 14

Atsumi
5 Healing

Th Sai
Yuan

13

20

17

16
15 18
Th Viset
Phuket Art Village

26 4
22
25

23
21

Hat Rawai
Boat
Charters

Th Viset

Ao Rawai

Ao Nai 1
Han

Hat Nai
Han

3

2

Hat Ya Nui

Laem
Phromthep

Rawai

Phuket
Paradise 4WD Tour

10

4233

4233

Secret View Point

Ko Man

Laem
Phromthep

12 24

Ao Sane

Th Viset

For reviews see	
◆ Top Experiences	p74
◎ Experiences	p77
✖ Eating	p79
🅗 Drinking	p82
🅔 Entertainment	p83

1 km
0.5 miles

N

Experiences

Hat Nai Han   BEACH

1 ⊚ Map p76, B3

Ask a local or expat here what their favourite beach is and they should tell you Hat Nai Han. Although they'll probably send you off somewhere else and keep this one 'in the vault'. One of Rawai's great swimming spots (take care in low tide though as it gets a bit rocky), this is a beautifully curved bay with minimal development, backed by casuarina trees and a seafront temple, Wat Nai Han.

Hat Ya Nui   BEACH

2 ⊚ Map p76, C3

Tucked between Hat Nai Han and Laem Phromthep, where the road dips down to the sea, this lovely little cove has a healthy rock reef that's ideal for snorkelling. You'll have to watch your step to get into the ocean, but once there you'll want to stay awhile. This is the quintessential turquoise bay, with lush mountains behind and an island dominating the horizon. (Hwy 4233)

Secret View Point   VIEWPOINT

3 ⊚ Map p76, B3

If you're looking for a sunset spot that's similarly enchanting to Laem

INGOLF POMPE/GETTY IMAGES ©

Hat Nai Han

Phromthep, but prefer things a bit more mellow away from the tour buses, then this is your place. To get here take Hwy 4233 to the top of the hill, where there is a turn-off.. (Hwy 4233)

Phuket Art Village
ART GALLERY

4 Map p76, C2

A group of talented Rawai-based artists have joined forces to set up this new village off the main strip. Expected to have been completed at the end of 2012, it will feature seven galleries including the Red Gallery and Love Art, which have relocated here. Plans are afoot to hold a monthly events day, the first Saturday of every month, with live music, food, art, a bar and puppet shadowplays to encourage families in the community to come together. (☏08 9471 5653, 08 7890 3722; Soi Naya 2; admission free; ☺10am-7pm)

Atsumi Healing
SPA

5 Map p76, D1

Phuket doesn't have to be all about boozing and eating creamy curries. Atsumi isn't just a spa, it's an earthy fasting and detox retreat centre. Most guests come to fast on water, juice and/or herbs for days at a time. Otherwise just pop in for a massage; either get the signature ThaiAtsu massage (think Thai meets shiatsu) or traditional Thai, oil and deep-tissue treatments. Meditative and gentle yoga classes with a touch of t'ai chi are also available. (☏08 1272 0571; www.

atsumihealing.com; 34/18 Soi Pattana; spa treatments from 1000B)

Phuket Shooting Range Complex
ADVENTURE SPORTS

6 Map p76, E1

You'll feel like Tom Hanks in *Big* at this 'playground' for adults that has archery, go-karting, ATV adventures and paintball spread out across the complex, just off Th Viset. (☏0 7638 1667; www.phuket-shooting.com; 82/2 Th Patak; go-karting per 10 mins from 890B; shooting gallery 10 shots from 790B; ☺9am-6pm)

Rawai Muay Thai
THAI BOXING

7 Map p76, D1

Strap up those wrists, pull on the gloves and get ready to rumble in the jungle at this Thai kick-boxing gym opened by a former *moo•ay tai* (also *muay thai*) champion. People come from around the world to learn how to fight alongside professional Thai fighters – it's a mix of locals and foreigners who live in on-site dorms, but tourists are welcome to drop in for lessons. (☏08 1476 9377; www.rawaimuaythai.com; 43/42 Moo 7, Th Sai Yuan; half-day training 300B)

Boat Charters
WATER SPORTS

8 Map p76, D3

The reason you've come to Phuket is to laze, snorkel and explore tropical islands, so it's lucky Rawai is a great base to do all this; charter a boat to the neighbouring islands for the day. (Th Viset, Hat Rawai)

Kite Zone
WATER SPORTS

9 Map p76, E1

With locations in Nai Yang and Rawai, this is the younger, hipper of the two kiteboarding schools, with a tremendous perch on Friendship Beach. Courses range in length from an hour to five days. (☎08 3395 2005; www.kitesurfingphuket.com; 1hr beginner lessons from 1100B; ☻May–late-Oct)

Phuket Paradise 4WD Tour
OUTDOORS

10 Map p76, B1

As passenger or driver, you can 4WD on dirt roads through the jungles of Phuket. Tours last either one or two hours and price includes hotel transfers. (☎0 7628 8501; 24/1 Moo 1, Hwy 4233; tours from 2300B; ☻8.30am-5.30pm)

Q Local Life

Wat Chalong

Tourists head to Rawai for the transcendental sunsets, but you can see how the locals attain Nirvana by stopping in at the bustling **Wat Chalong** (Hwy 4021; admission by donation). This tiered temple has 36 Buddhas seated, reclining and meditating on the first two floors. Concrete serpents line the banisters and the lotus pond outside. It's not an antique, but it possesses a spiritual vibration, especially when worshippers pay their respects.

Phuket Riding Club
ADVENTURE SPORTS

11 Map p76, E1

The perfect opportunity to fulfil that fantasy TV moment of riding a horse on the beach, Phuket Riding Club offers one-hour (per person 800B) and two-hour (1500B) rides in the jungle around Rawai and along nearby beaches. (☎0 7628 8213; www.phuketriding club.com; 95 Th Viset)

Ao Sane
BEACH

12 Map p76, B2

From Hat Nai Han it appears as if the road dead-ends into the yacht club. Not true. Keep following the road through the underground parking structure and it pops out on the other side and continues to a small but beautiful boulder-strewn white-sand beach. (Moo 1, north of Royal Phuket Yacht Club; admission free)

Eating

Rum Jungle
INTERNATIONAL $$$

13 Map p76, D1

One of Rawai's finest, this open-air thatched-roof restaurant is family run and spearheaded by a terrific Aussie chef. It's popular with the expat brigade; with New Zealand lamb shanks, steamed clams and eggplant parmigiana, you can see why. (☎0 7638 8153; 69/8 Th Sai Yuan; meals 300B-500B; ☻dinner Mon-Sat)

Baan Rimlay   THAI $$

14 Map p76, D3

The Thai seafood house to the right of the pier steams clams, mussels and fish, and grills squid, prawns and lobster to perfection. The seafood is a bit pricier here than at the more humble seafood joints down the street, but the location is superb and the views exceptional. (Th Viset, Hat Rawai; mains 120-650B; ⏰10am-10pm)

Da Vinci   ITALIAN $$

15 Map p76, C1

Alfresco wining and dining on crisp white linen-covered tables at this modern Italian kitchen is perfect on a balmy night. Ask for the deliciously authentic wood-fired porcini pizza made with imported ingredients. There's a play area for those with young ones in tow, and homemade Italian ice cream to keep a smile on their face, and yours. (☎0 7628 9574;

www.davinciphuket.com; 28/46 Moo 1, Th Viset; mains 230-800B; ⏰5.30-10.30pm)

Banana Corner   THAI $

16 Map p76, C1

Exquisite Royal Thai dishes served in a lush, twinkling, tropical garden. The rich panang curry is one of the best we've ever had. (☎0 7628 9045; www.bananacorner.net; 43/47 Th Viset; mains 80-380B; ⏰11am-midnight)

Kitchen Grill   THAI $

17 Map p76, D2

A cutesy white fence and chequered tablecloths give this tasty kitchen an inviting homely feel. Run by a young Thai family, it serves all-day breakfasts and great-value Thai lunch sets. If you're in need of a red-meat injection, order from the selection of Aussie steaks with your choice of garlic butter or pepper sauce. (☎08 1077 0853; Th Viset; mains 90-295B; ⏰8am-10pm)

Crepes Village   FRENCH $$

18 Map p76, C2

A pebbled garden with wooden gazebos lit by fairy lights, this family-friendly French-owned restaurant serves delicious French/Thai fusion crêpes. You'll find classics such as chamonix (egg, ham and cheese) but go with a local twist of green-curry-chicken filled crêpes or *panang goong* (prawns with panang curry paste, coconut milk and basil). They all go down very well with a biting French

---

Local Life
Rawai's Seafood Grills

More than a dozen **grill huts** (Map p76, D3; Th Viset, Hat Rawai; ⏰11am-10pm) line Rawai's beach road, and it doesn't much matter which one you choose. All the fish is fresh; the clams, mussels, prawns and lobster are not to be overlooked either. Make sure you try the spicy sauce, not that sweet and sour syrup. The prices are so good you will be stunned.

LONELY PLANET/GETTY IMAGES ©

Rawai Muay Thai (p78)

cider. *Bon appétit!* (☎08 5655 7329; www.crepesvillage.com; 28/31 Moo 1 Soi Saiyuan; mains 140-230B; ⏰7.30am-midnight)

Chalong Night Market   THAI $

19 🍴 Map p76, E1

One of the most popular night markets on the island. Vendors, farmers and local chefs converge under the gas lamps. Bring an appetite (that pumpkin curry looks good) and a shopping bag – it's always nice to have a mango in the morning. (Hwy 402, just north of Chalong Circle; ⏰6-11pm Wed)

German Bakery   EUROPEAN $

20 🍴 Map p76, D1

This friendly restaurant run by a German–Thai couple has the best

pastries in the area. It also makes a mean chicken schnitzel sandwich, serves delicious breakfasts, and has great currywurst. The food is simple, but always very good. (☎08 4843 3288; Th Viset; ⏰7.30am-5.30pm)

Oyjoi Number 1 Thai Food   THAI $

21 🍴 Map p76, C2

Don't let humble roots fool you. This delightful garden cafe run out of the chef's front yard serves some of the best Thai food in Phuket. The spicy panang curry, clotted with coconut cream, and the tamarind prawns – sticky but not too sweet – are our favourites, but it's all delicious. (☎08 9908 8808; 83/40 Moo 2, Th Viset; ⏰10am-10pm)

Living Food Cafe

VEGAN **$$**

22 Map p76, C2

When a 60-plus-year-old naturopath/ soul surfer extols raw food virtues and backs it up with a 2008 Ironman triathlon trophy, you listen. When he serves food so tasty and imaginative you forget how healthy it is, you ask for more. Dishes are free of wheat, sugar, dairy and animal products, but don't let that put you off. Comfort food in its raw form – burgers, tacos and lasagne – have to be seen and eaten to be believed. (☑08 1677 4555; Th Viset; ☉noon-2pm & 6-10pm)

M&M's Pizzeria

ITALIAN **$$**

23 Map p76, C2

Simply put, this is easily the best pizzeria on the island. The slightly sour crust is thin but with ample integrity, and its pastas and salads are tasty, too. (☑08 7272 3566, 08 1569 0244; Th Viset; pizzas from 240B; ☉6-11pm)

Drinking

Nikita's

BAR

Nestled on the seafront near Rawai pier, Nikita's (see **14** Map p76, D3) is the kind of place where you lose track of time thanks to the sea breezes, cocktails and chilled-out atmosphere. Anytime of day looks good here but balmy nights with the sand between your toes are just what you came here for, right? It also serves good watering-hole food such as burgers

and wood-fired pizzas. (☑0 7628 8703; Hat Rawai; ☉10am-late)

Royal Phuket Yacht Club

BAR

24 Map p76, B2

Sailing flags flap in the ocean breeze, waves pound the rocks below and there's nothing in sight but island views from the patio of the former Royal Meridian Yacht Club. It'll have you thinking you're in Monaco, minus the blazers and Maseratis, and is a location that demands a beverage, so order an ice-cold beer or fancy cocktail and watch the sun go down over the Andaman Sea. (☑0 7638 0200; www.theroyalphuketyachtclub.com; 23/3 Moo 1; ☉9am-midnight)

Reggae Bar

BAR

25 Map p76, C2

Spilling out from an old wooden shed and into a dirt lot is this wonderfully cluttered lounge, ringing with classic roots tunes. A leathersmiths by day, it hosts impromptu jams and (almost) monthly concerts and barbecues, featuring some of Thailand's most legendary Rastas, including Job2Do. DayGlo graffiti covers every inch of wall and floor space. (☑08 1273 5247; Th Viset; ☉noon-late)

Lavinier Coffee

CAFE

26 Map p76, C2

This local version of Starbucks (logo look familiar?) is an ideal spot to chill out for a while over good coffee made from ground Arabica beans sourced

Understand
Road Safety

- - - - - - - - - - - - - - -

Renting a motorbike or scooter can be a high-risk proposition in Phuket. If you must rent one, make sure you at least know the basics and wear a helmet, don't ride under the influence and wear appropriate clothing. Check your travel insurance carefully to ensure you're covered.

There have been recent late-night motorbike muggings and stabbings; the most common ambush spot is on Hwy 4233 between Karon View Point and Rawai. Over the last two years at least six robberies have taken place where solo motorbike riders were pushed off their bikes and then robbed. All of the attacks happened after midnight, so avoid driving in the wee hours.

from Chiang Mai. Thai/Croatian run, it also serves homemade traditional Bosnian breads as well as other European pastry favourites. (15/39 Moo 1, Th Viset; ⊙6am-11pm; 🛜)

Freedom Pub   PUB

27 🚇 Map p76, D3

Upon first glance it looks like a typical bar-girl haunt, but it really is a good tropical dive bar that both men and women will enjoy. The staff is friendly, there's a bar inside and a wonderful circle bar outside, and it has live music most nights. (📞0 7628 7402; Th Viset; ⊙2pm-2am)

Entertainment

Laguna Nightclub   NIGHTCLUB

28 ⭐ Map p76, D2

One of the few late-night spots in Rawai, Laguna Nightclub is set over two clubs opposite each other on a side street off Th Viset. It doesn't get going until the wee hours but heaves on weekend nights and attracts a mixed crowd of Thais and foreigners (and bar girls after knock-off), who sit around the several bars knocking back cocktails, playing pool and showcasing their drunken dance moves. (www.laguna-rawai.com; off Th Viset; no cover charge; ⊙11pm-late)

Explore

Hat Kamala & Hat Surin

Providing the perfect antidote to the madness of Patong, the neighbouring beaches of Kamala (pictured above) and Surin feature magnificent turquoise waters with gentle shore breakers to lull you to sleep in your deckchair. They attract a longer-term, lower-key guest, well suited to families and young couples. Despite recent luxury development, it remains grounded by beachfront seafood shacks and rustic bars.

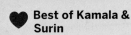

JAMES WAGHORN/GETTY IMAGES ©

The Region in a Day

Enjoy a sleep in and take advantage of the all-day breakfast at **Live Present Moment** (p89) before claiming your turf on the sand – book a chair from a local vendor or splash out at the chic **Catch Beach Club** (p87).

Give your skin a break from the scorching midday sun, and grab yourself a homemade gelato from **Bocconcinos** (p91) before getting a massage, and then retreat for a cold drink at the hidden away **Skyla's Beach House** (p92). Or if you want to get your blood pumping, trying some parasailing or rent a board and go for a paddle.

Head back to the beach for a late-afternoon dip, before freshening up and enjoying an evening show at the bizarre **Phuket Fantasea** (p88). Finish up at the **Beach Club Bar** (p92) with wine and cocktails.

♥ Best of Kamala & Surin

Drinking
Catch Beach Club (p87)

Skyla's Beach House (p87)

Dining
The Catch (p89)

Taste (p89)

Getting There

🚗 **Taxi** Private taxi from the airport to Surin/Kamala costs 550/600B.

Túk-túk From Surin to Kamala costs 150B; from Patong to Surin/Kamala costs 500/400B.

Sŏrngtăaou From Phuket Town to Surin/Kamala costs 30/35B; from Patong to Surin/Kamala costs 45/50B.

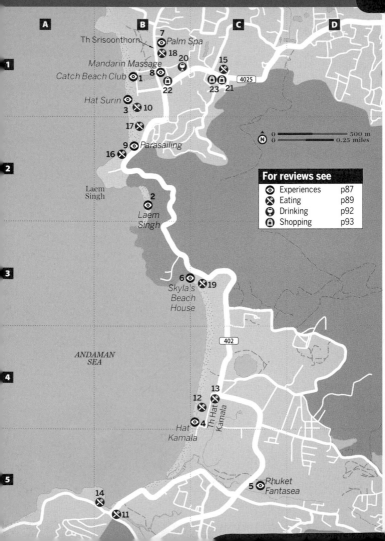

Th Srisoonthorn

7 Palm Spa
18
20
Mandarin Massage
15
Catch Beach Club 1
8
22
23 21
4025

Hat Surin
3 10

17

9 Parasailing
16

Laem
Singh

2

Laem
Singh

6
19
Skyla's
Beach
House

402

ANDAMAN
SEA

13
12
Th Hat Kamala
4
Hat
Kamala

14

11

5 Phuket
Fantasea

For reviews see

⊙	Experiences	p87
✗	Eating	p89
🍷	Drinking	p92
🔒	Shopping	p93

N
0   500 m
0   0.25 miles

Experiences

Catch Beach Club

BEACH CLUB

1 Map p86, B1

There's a day at the beach, and then there's a day at the beach, so forgo the towel on the sand and treat yourself to a day lazing in luxury on a plush cushioned beach bed. It's not cheap, but entry here buys you unlimited food and drink (or up to 5000B), and will make Surin's sands appear that bit whiter and the water that more azure. It's excellent value in the lower season months. (🕿 0 7631 6567; www.catchbeach club.com; Hat Surin; day pass low/high season 1500/5000B; ⏰ 9am-10.30pm; 🅿️)

Laem Singh

BEACH

2 Map p86, B2

Local beach goers will tell you that Laem Singh is one of the best capes on the island. Walled in by cliffs, there's no road access so you have to park on the headland and clamber down a narrow path. If you're renting a motorbike, it's is a nice little trip down Rte 4025 and then over dirt roads from Surin to Kamala.

Hat Surin

BEACH

3 Map p86, B1

Sassy and stylish, Surin is the beach where resort-goers come to play. Despite this, it remains unpretentious

Laem Singh

with its village vibe, and is a great spot for a day at the beach.

Hat Kamala BEACH

4 Map p86, C4

The next beach north from Hat Patong, Kamala is a long stretch of sand in a well-enclosed bay. Its rustic feel will suit those looking for a more mellow option to Patong.

Phuket Fantasea THEATRE

5 Map p86, C5

Phuket's original over-the-top cheesy extravaganza combines the colour and pageantry of Thai dance with state-of-the-art light-and-sound techniques to rival Las Vegas. Kids especially will be captivated by the spectacle which includes 30 performing elephants; animal activists on the other hand will be appalled. Arrive an hour earlier to wander the grounds and take in an atmosphere that's part Disneyland, part acid flashback, complete with Siberian tigers. (☏0 7638 5000; www.phuket-fantasea.com; admission with/without dinner 1900/1500B; ⊙shows 7pm & 9pm Wed & Fri, 9pm only Sat-Tue)

Skyla's Beach House SURFING

6 Map p86, B3

The best way for beginners to get out to Kamala's fun beach breaks is to get in touch with Skyla's Beach House on the northern end of the beach. Lessons are given by expert surfers, kids' lessons are free when accompanied by an adult, and hotel pick-up can be arranged. When it's flat in Kamala or Surin, they'll take you elsewhere. Also rents out stand-up paddleboards. (☏08 2519 3282; www.skylaphuket.com; Hat Kamala)

Palm Spa SPA

7 Map p86, B1

Pamper yourself with a yoghurt-and-coffee body scrub, coconut-cream bath and/or a hot-stone massage at this luxury spa on the main drag. It also has a full range of beauty services. The VIP room is a wonderful place for couples to splurge, featuring a rose-petal bath. (☏0 7631 6500; www.twinpalms-phuket.com; 106/46 Moo 3, Th Srisoonthorn; treatments from 850B; ⊙noon-8.30pm)

Local Life
Masjid Mukaram Bang Tao

While by no means a must-see sight, a visit to this **mosque** (Map p86, C1) on the busy Hwy 4025 nevertheless makes for an interesting change of scene from the beach. Its white facade and sea-green mosaic domes make for a striking image against the blue sky and jungled hills. It provides a good insight to Phuket village life, and is home to a friendly Muslim population who set up food carts outside the mosque selling tasty halal street food.

Mandarin Massage   SPA

8 ◉ Map p86, B1

An inexpensive massage option in
clean, air-conditioned surrounds,
with a menu offering Thai massage or
one with aloe vera for those who've
scorched themselves in the sun.
(www.mandarinphuket.com; 106/38 Moo 3
Srisoonthorn Rd; from 500B; ⊙9.30am-11pm)

Parasailing   WATER SPORTS

9 ◉ Map p86, B2

Fly high above stunning Surin with a
parasailing trip. (Hat Surin; per trip 1500B)

Eating

The Catch   FUSION $$$

While the idea of a buffet may not
inspire great confidence, the one at
the Catch (see 1 ◉ Map p86, B1) is worth
unbuckling your belt for. Gorge on all-
you-can-eat rock lobster, Aussie lamb
roasted on the spit and French oysters
while enjoying the beachside decking
and a bottle of crisp rosé. Bookings
are highly recommended for dinner.
(✆0 7631 6567; www.catchbeachclub.com;
Hat Surin; buffet from 1190B; ⊙9am-
10.30pm, buffet dinners Mon, Tue & Fri; 🛜🚼)

Taste   FUSION $$

10 ✕ Map p86, B1

The best of a new breed of urban-
meets-surf eateries along the beach.
Dine indoors or alfresco from an
ever-evolving menu. Choose from

Phuket Fantasea

WIBOWO RUSLI/GETTY IMAGES ©

meal-sized salads, perfectly cooked
fillet mignon, grilled fish tacos, and a
variety of Thai–Mediterranean start-
ers and mains. Service is outstanding
and there's an enticing attached gallery selling Tibetan, Nepali and local
jewellery and art. (✆08 7886 6401; www.
tastesurinbeach.com; tapas 190-375B; 🛜)

Live Present Moment   CAFE $$

11 ✕ Map p86, B5

Bringing cafe culture to Kamala, this
inviting spot succeeds not only in
all-day breakfast cook-ups and strong
coffee, but also excellent Thai food
and a classy interior courtesy of Jim
Thompson silk fabric. What really

Parasailing (p89)

lures people here are the fresh rice-paper-wrapped Vietnamese rolls filled with chicken or prawns. (16/15 Moo 6 Rim Hard; ☺closed Wed)

Deng's
INTERNATIONAL, THAI **$**

12 ✗ Map p86, C4

A loved, long-time favourite, Deng's is a friendly and relaxed open-air eatery with the best food on this end of the beach. You can get your pasta, burgers and Wiener schnitzel here, but you'd be better served by ordering the local seafood. A buffet barbecue is held every Wednesday from 8pm. Enjoy! (☎0 7638 5981; Soi Police Station; ☺8am-10pm)

Nanork Seafood
THAI **$$**

13 ✗ Map p86, C4

A charming stone-and-timber seafood restaurant with a daily mixed-grill selection and blooming flowers on tables nestled in the sand. (94/19 Moo 3; ☺8am-11pm)

Rockfish
FUSION **$$**

14 ✗ Map p86, B5

Perched above the river mouth and the bobbing long tails, with beach, bay and mountain views, Rockfish boasts prime real estate. Smoked-salmon eggs Benedict on English muffins for breakfast, garlic-and-pepper-infused fish and chips for lunch, and five-spiced pork loin with crackling and roast potatoes for dinner are all temptations hard to resist. Also has an entire separate menu for vegetarians (📞 0 7627 9732; www.rockfishrestaurant.com; 33/6 Th Kamala Beach; dishes 150-1000B; 🕐breakfast, lunch & dinner; 📶🍴)

Bocconcino
ITALIAN, DELI **$$**

15 🍴 Map p86, C1

Sure, an Italian deli may not be what you've come to Phuket for, but until you've tasted the homemade gelato then you haven't experienced Surin. The pistachio and creamy fig taste like they've just been plucked off the tree. It's a true blessing in this climate. As is the icy air-con, which houses an Italophile's dream of wines, coffee, cheeses, cured meats, homemade pastas, paninis and dishes such as slow-cooked lamb shanks in red wine. (Hwy 4025, 8/71 Moo 3; 🕐9am-6pm; 📶)

Patcharin Seafood
THAI **$**

16 🍴 Map p86, B2

One of the first fish grills to open along Hat Surin, Patcharin is a large open-air bamboo shack at the southernmost end of the beach, known for its extensive menu of seafood, barbecued meats and Thai curries. (Hat Surin; 🕐8.30am-10pm)

Pla Seafood
AUSTRIAN, THAI **$$**

Pla (see **10** 🍴 Map p86, B1) delivers the unlikely pairing of Thai and Austrian cuisine, which means you can have your barbecued squid and steamed crab with Wiener schnitzel, amid a stylish beach setting of cane chairs

and glass-top tables on the sand. Also hires sun loungers for 300B. (📞 0 7632 5572; www.plaseafood.com; Hat Surin; mains 250-1000B; 🕐8am-11pm)

Twin Brothers
THAI **$**

17 🍴 Map p86, B2

By day, one brother mans the wok, stirring up decent Thai food at local prices. At night, the other fires up a fresh seafood grill for beachside diners. (Hat Surin; 🕐10.30am-10.30pm)

Weaves
FUSION **$$**

18 🍴 Map p86, B1

Set in a gorgeous atrium with flowing fountains, a lotus pond and old timber floors is this appetising fusion restaurant attached to the Manathai resort. Grilled salmon with an assortment of coconutty Thai dips, or crispy soft shell crab with black pepper are what you can expect here. Also does good burgers and sandwiches for lunch. (📞 0 7627 0900; 121/1 Th Srisoonthorn; mains 200-400B; 🕐11am-10.30pm; 📶)

Ma Ma Fati Ma
THAI **$**

19 🍴 Map p86, C3

This beachfront snack-shack is a real find. The family who owns and operates it could not be more welcoming. The tasty Thai food is exceptional and so are the fresh fruit shakes. (far north end of Hat Kamala)

Drinking

Skyla's Beach House
BAR

In the face of some serious five-star development, this old-school rustic bamboo bar keeps things real. Perched upon rickety stilts on a rocky cove at the northern end of Kamala beach, chilled-out Skyla's (see 6 ◎ Map p86, B3) is your classic end-of-the-road paradise hideaway, making it a great spot to lazily sip on a cold drink while gazing out to the ocean. It also serves Thai food and offers surfing lessons. (www.skylaphuket.com; Hat Kamala; ⊙11am-8pm)

Beach Club Bar
BAR

This chic outdoor beachside lounge with faux-leather chairs, attached to the Catch Beach Club (see 1 ◎ Map p86, B1), is the place to be seen in Surin. The decking bar is centered under a sleek sail and is the kind of place you'd go for a bucket of ice and champagne to enjoy that perfect sunset. There's also fire twirling and other theatrics to get the party started. (www.catchbeachclub.com; 88/4 Th Hat Nai Yang, Hat Surin; ⊙10am-2am; ☏)

Liquid Lounge

20 ⬤ Map p86, B1

A stylish, loft-style martini lounge with premium liquor, occasional live

---

Understand
Moo•ay Tai

Moo•ay tai (Thai boxing; also spelled *muay thai*) is both Thailand's indigenous martial art and the nation's favourite sport. What captivates is its emphasis on close-quarters fighting. Fighters use their knees, elbows, feet and fists to inflict damage.

In 1774, when Myanmar (Burma) briefly ruled Thailand, the impulsive Burmese king held a seven-day, seven-night religious festival in honour of Lord Buddha. Overcome with a very un-Buddhist impulse, he wanted to see some blood during the festivities. So he called upon Nai Khanom Tom, a Thai prisoner of war and a *moo•ay tai* expert, to fight a Burmese swordsman.

Nai Khanom Tom did a traditional Wai Kru prefight dance, which loosens up the fighter and honours the teacher, and in this case, the Burmese king. He then crushed his opponent. Baffled, the king made him fight another Burmese champion, and another. All told, Tom fought and defeated nine fighters in a row. He won his freedom (and two Burmese wives) that night.

Originally *moo•ay tai* was taught in the military, but the Buddhist monasteries inherited stewardship, which helps explain why even today's fighters live like monks.

jazz and wi-fi. (☎08 1537 2018; Th Hat Surin; ⏰4pm-1am; 🛜)

Shopping

Lemongrass House　　BEAUTY

Phuket's best producer of all-natural health and beauty products, Lemongrass's (see 8 ◎ Map p86, B1) shelves are packed with creams, lotions, scrubs, masks, essential oils, shampoos and washes made from all-natural materials – mostly using its namesake ingredient. The homemade chunky bars of soap have scents ranging from cucumber or fig tea to virgin coconut, and all smell divine. Oh, and that nontoxic mosquito repellent really does the job. (☎0 7627 1233; www.lemongrasshouse.com; Th Hat Surin; ⏰9am-8pm)

Island Bliss　　CLOTHING

21 🔒 Map p86, C1

Specialising in 'resort' wear ranging from long, flowing cotton dresses in classy fine prints and swimwear to patchwork totebags. All clothes and accessories are designed by an Australian woman whose inspiration spans from India and Bali to Byron Bay. (www.islandblissphuket.com; Hwy 4025)

Oriental Fine Art　　ART

22 🔒 Map p86, B1

One of the best collections of traditional Asian art in Thailand, this museum-quality showroom features Buddhas, including a 3m Buddha encrusted with precious stones, an ancient teak shrine and the like. Some pieces are for sale; others are just for show. Also has the Art of Living sister branch up the road. (☎0 7632 5141; Th Hat Surin; ⏰9am-9pm)

Soul of Asia　　ART

23 🔒 Map p86, C1

A lovely gallery filled with fine, funky Southeast Asian modern and traditional art, mixed with original prints and lithographs from masters such as Picasso, Dalí, Miró and Warhol. Art lovers will want to stop in for a look even if you're not in the market. (☎0 7627 0055; www.soulofasia.com; 5/50 Moo 3, Hwy 4025, Surin Plaza; ⏰10.30am-7.30pm)

Explore

Ao Bang Thao

Following the length of Ao Bang Thao's stunning, long white sand is a journey into the island's psyche. It starts off as a local fishing village, before food shacks morph into swanky beach clubs. Then comes the Laguna Phuket complex of five-star resorts, before mother nature, thankfully, asserts herself with a lonely stretch of powder-white sand and tropical blue.

The Region in a Day

☼ Ao Bang Thao is all about doing nothing. There are no real pesky 'sights' to get you out of bed early here, so have a lie in and then amble your way down to **Hat Bang Thao** (p97) for a morning dip in the sea and to soak up some sun. Once you start getting peckish, head over to the **Family Restaurant** (p97) for some good North Indian curries or opt for Thai and beachfront views at the **Andaman Restaurant** (p97).

☼ Spend the whole afternoon relaxing on your rattan sun lounger at the **Bliss Beach Club** (p97) (which you booked the day before), being waited on hand and foot, sipping cocktails under casuarina trees and deciding between swimming in the sea or the pool.

☾ Treat yourself to a gourmet meal at the **Babylon Beach Club** (p97). From one beach club to another, this is the life! Drink into the night to a Rasta soundtrack at the **Reggae Bar** (p99).

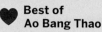 **Best of Ao Bang Thao**

Dining
Bliss Beach Club (p97)

Babylon Beach Club (p97)

Andaman Restaurant (p97)

Relaxing
Bliss Beach Club (p97)

Ao Bang Thao (p97)

Getting There

🚗 **Taxi** Private taxi from the airport costs 200B to 300B.

Túk-túk Charters from southern beaches cost around 700B.

Sŏrngtăaou From Phuket Town costs 25B.

ANDAMAN SEA

Th Laguna

Hat Bang Thao

8

6
3

2

Th Hat Bang Thao

Ao Bang Thao

Bliss Beach Club

1

5

4

CHOENG THALEH

7

For reviews see

Experiences	p97
Eating	p97
Drinking	p99

0   500 m
0   0.25 miles

Experiences

Bliss Beach Club
BEACH CLUB

1 ◉ Map p96, B4

As if Ao Bang Thao beach wasn't blissful enough, this club offers a five-star beach experience. Chill-out tunes play softly in the background as guests sit around reading books, sipping drinks or watching their kids splash in the pool. Smartly uniformed staff, in retro Beach Boys stripe style, serve drinks and some of the best food on the island to tables on the large beachside deck, shaded by casuarina trees. (☑0 7651 0150; www.blissbeachclub.com; 202/88 Moo 2; ⊙11am-late; ⊞)

Hat Bang Thao
BEACH

2 ◉ Map p96, B2

One of the longest beaches on the island, Bang Thao mixes luxury resorts at one end and not much else at the other. Its soft white sand is just asking for you to lie around on it and do nothing.

Eating

Bliss Beach Club
INTERNATIONAL $$

Even if you don't commit to a day indulging in its plush surrounds, try to stop in here (see **1** ◉ Map p96, B4) for lunch. The menu of garlic prawn Neapolitan-style pizza, fresh crunchy baguettes and delicious chocolate mousse is served with gorgeous sea views. Sunday brunch from 1pm attracts a young party crowd and gets busy, so book ahead. (☑0 7651 0150; www.blissbeachclub.com; 202/88 Moo 2; ⊙11am-late)

Babylon Beach Club
ITALIAN, THAI $$$

3 ✕ Map p96, C2

Accessible by dirt road are the polished, whitewashed, seaside environs of the Babylon Beach Club, specialising in Italian cuisine. Lunch is more casual 'beach fare' such as burgers and salads, while dinner gets more lavish. (☑08 1970 5302; Hat Bang Thao; dishes 120-850B; ⊙10am-10.30pm)

Andaman Restaurant
THAI $$

4 ✕ Map p96, B4

Part of the Andaman Seaside Resort, this simple restaurant on the sand has a lovely castaway paradise feel with rustic thatched umbrellas, bamboo lanterns and driftwood furniture. Dine on barbecue seafood and Thai curries right by the water's edge. (69/74, Moo 3 Hat Bang Thao; mains 120-250B; ⊙7am-10pm; 🛜)

The Family Restaurant
INDIAN $

5 ✕ Map p96, C4

While most eateries in Phuket try to cover all cuisine bases, this one stays true to its Indian menu with a good selection of tandoori and North Indian curries. The thatched-roof bamboo shack facade opens to a bright airy place with a Bollywood soundtrack and tables covered in

Understand

Pop's Culture: Life as a Ladyboy

Pop, aged 45, is what Thais call a *gà•teu•i*, usually referred to as a 'lady-boy' in English.

Why does there seem to be so many gà•teu•i in Thailand? Most think that there are tonnes of ladyboys in Thailand because they're in places that many tourists visit. Yes, some ladyboys want to be cabaret dancers, just like some women want to be cabaret dancers, but most don't. These types of jobs are the only ones available, and the pay is lousy. Life is not as 'Hollywood' as it may seem on stage. Since many of us cannot have proper jobs, many don't bother going to school. I feel like a second-class citizen; we're not allowed to use male or female bathrooms! I used to have to climb 14 flights of stairs to use the special ladyboys' bathroom at my old job!

How does one tell the difference between a ladyboy and a woman on the street? Sometimes it's really hard to tell...sometimes a ladyboy can be more beautiful than a woman! Doctors are really starting to perfect the operations, and the operations are expensive –mine was 150,000B! I had the 'snip', breast implants, my Adam's apple was shaved off and a nose job. Other operations available include silicone implants in the hips, jaw narrowing, cheekbone shaving and chin sculpting. But before anyone can have an operation, you have to have a psych evaluation.

How has your family handled the transition? My mother was always very comforting. A month before my operation she told me 'you will always be my child, but never lie to anyone about who you are – accept who you are'. I have two adopted sons who are now quite grown-up, and after I made the change, they bought me presents on Mother's Day instead of Father's Day – I thought that was very sweet. My father on the other hand was never very supportive. When he found I was sleeping with men, he...well...let's put it this way, he practised his *moo•ay tai* boxing on me.

What was the first thing that passed through your mind when you woke up after the operation? I woke up with a big smile. Life is great. I am happy that I can be on the outside what I am on the inside.

Condensed interview, as told to Brandon Presser

Tik Restaurant

rainbow gingham cloth. (82/10-12 Moo 3; 50-200B; ☺1pm-midnight)

Tik Restaurant   THAI $$

6 🍴 Map p96, C2

Tik is among several local Thai restaurants on this stretch of beach specialising in fresh grilled seafood. (📞08 9475 5053; 41/6 Moo 3, Hat Bang Thao; 100-300B; ☺10am-11pm)

Nok & Jo's   THAI, INTERNATIONAL $$

7 🍴 Map p96, B4

On a quiet stretch of road sits this Canadian-owned ramshackle sports-bar-ranch-cum-restaurant serving an extensive mix of Thai and Western dishes. Heavily varnished driftwood furniture resembling giant unruly pretzels mixes with a hodge-podge of animal skulls, international flags, boating paraphernalia and licence plates. It's headache-inducing, sure, but the barbecue buffets on Wednesdays, Fridays & Sundays, and gà•teu•i (ladyboy) cabaret on Wednesdays and Sundays are good fun. (www.nokandjo. com; 8 Soi Haddsurin; mains 100-600B; ☺9am-late; 📶)

Drinking

Reggae Bar

8 🍸 Map p96, C2

Stroll down the beach to this tiki bar. Kick back and let Bob Marley soothe your soul. (Hat Bang Thao; ☺9am-late)

Explore

Thalang & Around

Phuket's northeastern hemisphere, once a film set for *Good Morning Vietnam*, is laced with temples, waterfalls, singing gibbons and adrenaline-stirring zip lines through lush jungle. Variety is the spice of life, so drag yourself off that beach lounger, and gear up for a day's adventure jaunting through the island's tropical rainforest.

The Region in a Day

☀ Arrive early to see **Wat Phra Thong** (p103; pictured left) in the early morning sun, before heading into **Khao Phra Thaew National Park** (p103) to spend some time learning about the gibbons at the **Phuket Gibbon Rehabilitation Centre** (p103). Arrange a guided walk at the park's entrance and take a few hours to explore the park on the pleasant walk between **Bang Pae Falls** (p103) and Ton Sai Falls. After all the action, you'll be starved so drop in at **Monkeypod** (p105) for a coffee and light lunch.

☀ Spend the afternoon at the interesting **Thalang National Museum** (p103) for a history lesson, then rouse yourself with an adrenaline hit, zip-lining through the jungle at **Cable Jungle Adventures** (p104).

☾ Things are pretty quiet around Thalang when the sun goes down. Make your way over to **Bang Rong** (p105) for a peaceful dinner to finish off the action-filled day, and watch the fishing boats come back in as you dine on freshly caught seafood.

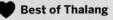 **Best of Thalang**

Sights

Khao Phra Thaew National Park (p103)

Phuket Gibbon Rehabilitation Centre (p103)

Bang Pae Falls (p103)

Cultural Experiences

Thalang National Museum (p103)

Wat Phra Thong (p103)

Getting There

Sŏrngtăaou From Phuket Town to Bang Rong costs 35B.

🚗 **Taxi** From Patong 300B or Kata/Karon costs 600B.

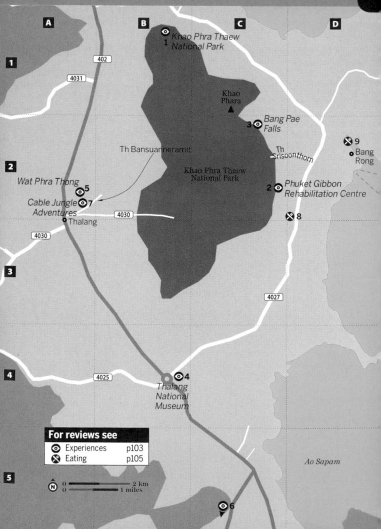

A

B Khao Phra Thaew
National Park
1

C

D

402

4031

Khao
Phara
▲

Bang Pae
Falls
3

Th
Srisoonthorn

9

Bang
Rong

Th Bansuanneramit

Khao Phra Thaew
National Park

2 Phuket Gibbon
Rehabilitation Centre

Wat Phra Thong

5

Cable Jungle
Adventures
7

Thalang

4030

8

4030

4027

4025

Thalang
National
Museum
4

Ao Sapam

6

For reviews see

◉ Experiences p103
✕ Eating p105

N 0 —————— 2 km
0 —————— 1 miles

Experiences

Khao Phra Thaew National Park
NATIONAL PARK

1 ⊙ Map p102, B1

Kick off your thongs and strap up those boots to hit the trails of Khao Phra Thaew's evergreen monsoon forest. The national park protects 23 sq km of virgin rainforest, and there are some pleasant hikes over the hills, particularly between the two waterfalls from Bang Pae Falls to Ton Sai. Go it alone or arrange a guide at the park's HQ at the entrance. The highest point in the park is Khao Phara (442m). (📞0 7631 1998; Hwy 4030; adult/child 200/100B)

Phuket Gibbon Rehabilitation Centre
WILDLIFE SANCTUARY

2 ⊙ Map p102, C2

A tiny sanctuary in the Khao Phra Taew park, this rehabilitation centre is open to the public although you can't see much of the gibbons in their cages from afar. Financed by donations (1500B will care for a gibbon for a year), the centre adopts gibbons that have been kept in captivity in the hope they can be reintroduced to the wild. (📞0 7626 0492; www.gibbonproject. org; ⊙9am-4.30pm)

Bang Pae Falls
WATERFALL

3 ⊙ Map p102, C2

In Khao Phra Taew National Park, this waterfall is a 300m walk up a jun-gled earth and concrete path from the gibbon rehab centre, and you'll hear their haunting songs from the rehab all the way. During the dry season, the waterfall isn't exactly spectacular, but there are swimming holes deep enough for daring jumps (check it's safe first though) and rocks for you to sit on and ponder. (access from Hwy 4027, Khao Phra Thaew National Park)

Thalang National Museum
MUSEUM

4 ⊙ Map p102, B4

Phuket's premier museum contains five exhibition halls chronicling southern themes such as the history of Thalang-Phuket and the colonisation of the Andaman coast. The prize artefact is a 2.3m-tall statue of Vishnu, which dates to the 9th century and was found in Takua Pa nearly 100 years ago. Outside the main entrance is the ramshackle tsunami exhibition hall of objects washed up on the island – currency exchange signs, typewriters and boat wreckage among them. There's no sign; take your first right off the Hwy. (📞0 7631 1426; Off Hwy 4027; admission 100B; ⊙9am-4.30pm)

Wat Phra Thong
TEMPLE

5 ⊙ Map p102, A2

Phuket's 'Temple of the Gold Buddha' is half buried so that only the head and shoulders are visible above ground. According to local legend, those who have tried to excavate the image have become very ill or encountered serious accidents. The temple is particularly revered by Thai Chinese, many of whom believe the image hails from China. In addition to Phra Thong there are 11 other Buddha images, each promising a different virtue (success, health, wealth etc) to those who make offerings. (Off Hwy 402; admission by donation; ☉dawn-dusk)

Amazing Bike Tours

ADVENTURE SPORTS

6 ◉ Map p102, C5

Phuket's best new adventure outfitter, Amazing Bike Tours leads small groups on half-day bicycle tours through the Khao Phra Thaew National Park, and offers terrific day trips around Ko Yao Noi and the gorgeous beaches and waterfalls of Thai Muang in nearby Phang-Nga province. (☏0 7628 3436; www.amazingbiketoursthai land.asia; 32/4 Moo 9, Th Chaofa, Chalong; day trips from 1600B)

Cable Jungle Adventures

ADVENTURE SPORTS

7 ◉ Map p102, A2

Tucked into the hills behind a quilt of pineapple fields, rubber plantations and mango groves is this maze of eight zip lines linking cliffs to ancient ficus trees. The zips range from 6m to 23m above the ground and the longest run is 100m long. Closed-toe shoes are a must and free pick-up is included

Bang Pae Falls (p103)

Understand
Sisters Are Doin' It for Themselves – Thalang's Heroines

The untimely death of Thalang's governor in 1785 left Phuket in a vulnerable position as the fleet of invading Burmese troops set upon the island with no one to take charge. With no other choice but to take matters into their own hands, the governor's wife Kunying Jan and her sister, Mook, assembled the local forces and prepared for battle. Using cunning tactics to fool the Burmese army, the sisters called upon the residents of Phuket, including women, to dress up as soldiers so their military 'manpower' seemed invincible to the Burmese scouts. If this sounds familiar, you're thinking of the *Three Amigos*.

It was to prove a masterstroke move as the Burmese retreated after a short conflict, and the sisters became heroes and given honorary titles by King Rama I. Today they stand side by side immortalised, swords in hand, at the **Thalang Heroine Monument**, which most visitors to Phuket will pass at the roundabout on the way to and from the airport. They remain highly revered and a major festival is held annually on 13 March to commemorate their victory with re-enactments performed by a cast of a thousand.

from the beaches. (☎08 1977 4904; 232/17 Moo 8, Th Bansuanneramit; per person 1600B; ⊙9am-6pm)

Eating

Monkeypod   CAFE $
8 ✖ Map p102, D2

This hip, modern, family-run cafe is a welcome surprise when heading along Hwy 4027 en route to the gibbons, Thalang Museum or the national park. The coffee here is exceptional and the cafe has a leafy outlook with huge glass windows, cool white walls and tables made from monkeypod wood (trees that surround the area). The cafe food is also very good, with reasonably priced chicken wraps and other light lunches. (cnr Th Lum Sai & Hwy 4027; mains 80-120B; ⊙9am-9pm; ☎)

Bang Rong Seafood   THAI $
9 ✖ Map p102, D2

This rustic fish-farm-turned-restaurant is set on a floating pier in the mangroves. It has red and white snapper, crab and mussels, and it plucks your catch after you order, so you know it's fresh. You can have it steamed, fried or grilled, but it's a Muslim enterprise so you can't have beer. Come at sunset, when fishermen chat on the dock, and the light plays on both the water and the mangroves. It's a special scene. (Bang Rong pier; ⊙10am-10pm)

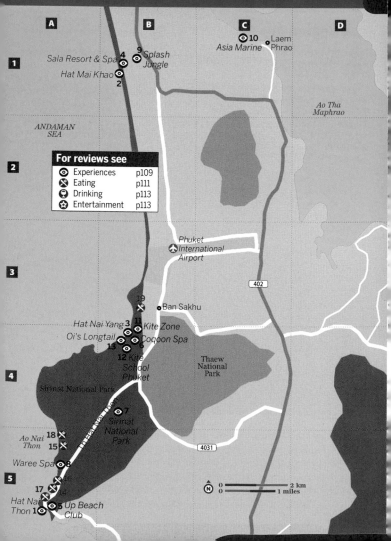

ANDAMAN
SEA

Ao Tha
Maphrao

For reviews see

◉	Experiences	p109
✖	Eating	p111
⬤	Drinking	p113
✪	Entertainment	p113

Sala Resort & Spa
Hat Mai Khao

4
9 Splash
Jungle
2

◉ 10
Asia Marine

Laem
Phrao

Phuket
International
Airport

402

19
Ban Sakhu

Hat Nai Yang 3
Oi's Longtail
13
12 Kite
School
Phuket

11
Kite Zone
Coqoon Spa

Sirinat National Park

7
Sirinat
National
Park

Thaew
National
Park

4031

Ao Nai
Thon
18
15

Waree Spa ◉ 8

17

Hat Nai
Thon 1 ◉ ◉ 5 Up Beach
Club

0   2 km
0   1 miles
N

Experiences

Hat Nai Thon
BEACH

1  Map p108, A5

If you're after a lovely arc of fine golden sand, away from the buzz of Phuket busyness, Hat Nai Thon is it. It's further south from Hat Nai Yang, and swimming is quite good here except at the height of the monsoon. It also has some decent snorkelling; be careful of treading on the coral near the headlands at either end of the bay.

Hat Mai Khao
BEACH

2 Map p108, B1

Phuket's longest beach is a beautiful secluded stretch of sand that you'll have all to yourself most of the time. Sea turtles lay their eggs here between November and February. Be aware of strong year-round undertow.

Hat Nai Yang
BEACH

3 Map p108, B4

In between Hat Nai Thon and Hat Mai Khao, the bay here is sheltered by a reef that slopes 20m below the surface – which makes for both good snorkelling in the dry season and fantastic surfing in the monsoon season.

Sala Resort & Spa
SPA

4 Map p108, B1

Feel like a celebrity at the hip and sexy, yet not full of itself, Sala Resort. The villa property is a blend of Sino-

Hat Nai Thon

Portuguese and art deco influences with a modern flair. Choose to be indulged with a body scrub and milk bath in your own private granite tub set in a pebbled courtyard, or opt for a beachfront massage. Couples' rooms available. (☏ 0 7633 8888; www.salaphuket. com; 333 Moo 3, Tambon Maikhao; treatments from 1800B; ⏰9am-9pm)

Up Beach Club
BEACH CLUB

5 Map p108, A5

At the southern end of Hat Nai Thon you'll find one of Phuket's most exclusive beach clubs, with its opulent Mediterranean feel, large decked terrace overlooking the Andaman Sea, private steps to the secluded beach and the kind of service usually only

VIPs can dream of. Closes in the low season. (☑ 08 0144 6635; www.upbeach club.com; Malaiwana, Hat Nai Thon; day pass 500B; ☺10am-10pm)

Coqoon Spa

SPA

6 ◉ Map p108, B4

Set in a 277-room megaresort at the Indigo Pearl, this is a fantastic spa where individual rooms are backed against lush tropical gardens and rainforest. Treatments include a purple frangipani scrub and a pearl wrap featuring vegetal extracts of local cultured pearls. (☑ 0 7632 7006; www. indigo-pearl.com; Hat Nai Yang; treatments from 2000B; ☺9am-9pm)

Sirinat National Park

NATIONAL PARK

7 ◉ Map p108, B4

The former Nai Yang National Park and Mai Khao wildlife reserve encompasses 22 sq km of coastal land, plus 68 sq km of sea. It runs from the western Phang-Nga provincial border south to the headland that separates Nai Yang from Nai Thon. The beach is absolutely pristine. Sea turtles patrol the reef and lay eggs on the park's northern beaches and on Hat Mai Khao. (☑ 0 7632 8226; www.dnp.go.th; admission 200B; ☺8am-5pm)

Waree Spa

SPA

8 ◉ Map p108, A5

The spa at this sweet family-owned cottage resort has basic but tasteful environs, a proper Scandinavian sauna and a variety of massages on the menu. (☑ 0 7620 5233; 22/2 Th Surin; massages from 400B; ☺7.30am-10pm, closed during the wet season)

Splash Jungle

AMUSEMENT PARK

9 ◉ Map p108, B1

The biggest water park in Thailand has a wave pool, a play pool with tipping buckets and water cannons, 12 very cool water slides for all ages, and a sauna and bar for mum and dad. The price includes pick-up at your resort. (☑ 0 7637 2111; www.splashjungle waterpark.com; Mai Khao; adult/5-12yr/under 5yr 1295/650B/free; ☺10am-6pm)

Sirinat National Park

Asia Marine
BOATING

10 Map p108, C1

One of the first yacht charters in Phuket and with the most diverse fleet cruising the Andaman Sea, Asia Marine has a boat for everyone – from sleek fibreglass catamarans to wooden junks. Reservations and enquiries are available online only. (www.asia-marine. net; Yacht Haven Phuket Marina)

Kite Zone
WATER SPORTS

11 Map p108, B4

Highly professional kiteboarding operator open from May to October. Also has a branch in Chalong Bay, which is open year-round. (☑ 08 1591 4594; www. kiteboardingasia.com; Th Beach; 3hr lessons from 4000B; ☉ May–late-Oct)

Kite School Phuket
WATER SPORTS

12 Map p108, B4

Long-established German-run kiteboarding outfit with friendly enthusiastic staff. It relocates to Chalong Bay for the alternate November to February season. (☑ 08 0077 7594; www. kiteschoolphuket.com; Th Beach; 3hr lessons from 3500B; ☉ May–late-Oct)

Oi's Longtail
SNORKELLING

13 Map p108, B4

Oi specialises in two-hour snorkelling tours of the reefs around Ko Waeo. Located at Bank Restaurant, opposite the long-tail boat harbour. (☑ 08 1978 5728; 66 Moo 3, Hat Nai Yang; tours 1600B)

Eating

Batik Seafood
THAI $

This beautiful beach-garden restaurant (see **13** Map p108, B4), nestled on the southern end of Hat Nai Yang just after the road turns to dust, sports tables beneath thatched gazebos and is surrounded by orchids. Batik Seafood specialises in fresh grilled fish, which it chooses from the fish market that is held just north of the restaurant every afternoon. (88/3 Th Hat Nai Yang; mains from 100B; ☉ 10.30am-10pm)

Chao Lay Bistro
THAI $$

14 Map p108, A5

Tasty Thai food in a hip, open-air dining room. Try the *panang thalay* – prawns or squid in red curry with lime leaves and coconut milk. (☑ 0 7620 5500; www.naithonburi.com; 9 Moo 4, Tambon Sakhu; mains from 150B; ☉ noon-10.30pm)

Mr Oody
THAI, INTERNATIONAL $

15 Map p108, A5

Mr Oody is a friendly beach restaurant on the sand. It mixes glass-top tables and white umbrellas with a great sunset location overlooking the rocky end of Hat Nai Thon. Fried lobster with chilli paste is a must from the extensive menu. Also does good breakfast sets and fresh-fruit shakes. (Hat Nai Thon; mains 80-380B; ☉ 8am-10pm)

Understand
The Marine Environment

Environmental Issues

Thailand's coral reef system, including the Andaman coast from Ranong to northern Phuket and the Surin and Similan Islands, is one of the world's most diverse. Some 600 species of coral reef fish, endangered marine turtles and other rare creatures call this coastline home. The 2004 tsunami caused high-impact damage to about 13% of the Andaman coral reefs; however, damage from the tsunami was much less than first thought and relatively minor compared to the ongoing environmental degradation that accompanies an industrialised society.

It is estimated that about 25% of Thailand's coral reefs have died as a result of industrial pollution and that the annual loss of healthy reefs will continue at a rapid rate. Even around the dive centre of Phuket, dead coral reefs are visible on the northern coast. The biggest threat to corals is sedimentation from coastal development: new hotels, roads and houses. High levels of sediment in the water stunt the growth of coral. Other common problems include pollution from anchored tour boats or other marine activities, rubbish and sewage dumped directly into the sea, and agricultural and industrial run-off. Even people urinating in the water as they swim creates by-products that can kill sensitive coral reefs.

Responsible Travel

It may be a holiday but travellers need to be responsible and do what they can do to minimise the impact of their visits, or to even make a positive impact. Walk along most of Phuket's beaches these days and it's hard to ignore the rubbish, particularly in high season. Students at Dulwich International College in Phuket collected 5000kg of rubbish from the beach in a single day; help them out by, firstly, throwing yours in the bin and, secondly, picking up rubbish whenever you can.

When swimming, diving or snorkelling, do not touch or walk on coral, monitor your movements so you avoid accidentally sweeping into coral, and do not harass marine life. Finally, don't urinate in the water – this is a no-brainer for loads of reasons, not least because it's disgusting.

Coconut Tree

THAI $

16 Map p108, A5

Plonk some chairs on the beach and you got yourself a restaurant. Dine with the sand between your toes at this relaxed spot serving fresh seafood dishes such as stir-fried crab with black pepper or prawn-dumpling soup. (Hat Nai Thon; mains from 100B; ☉11am-11pm; 🛜)

Tien Seng

THAI $

17 Map p108, A5

Cheap and tasty Thai food and decent American breakfasts are yours at the south end of the beach. It fires up the fish grill at night. (📞08 4948 1826; 28 Th Hat Nai Thon; mains from 80B; ☉8.30am-10.30pm)

Wiwan

THAI $

18 Map p108, A5

You can try local dishes, such as *yum koong siab* (southern-style smoked prawns), or exotic ones, such as vegie burgers. It also has a seafood barbecue in the evenings. (📞0 7620 5233; 22/2 Th Surin; dishes from 100B; ☉7.30am-10pm, closed during the wet season)

Bread & Butter

CAFE $

19 Map p108, B3

Part of the Dewa resort across from Hat Nai Yang, this tiny cafe is a good spot for your morning coffee and serves a range of homemade classic pies, freshly baked bread, sandwiches and bagels, and a selection of sweet treats like apple crumble or chocolate croissants. (📞0 7637 2300; 65 Moo 1, Hat Nai Yang; coffee from 100B; pies 148B; ☉7am-7pm)

Drinking

Mr Kobi

BAR

When the other beach shacks close, the gregarious Mr Kobi's (see **13** ◉ Map p108, B4) blender whirs on, and his kitchen doesn't close till the guests go home, or pass out. (Hat Nai Yang; ☉11am-1am)

Entertainment

The Beach Club

PUB

This beach pub (see **13** ◉ Map p108, B4) brings nightlife to sleepy Nai Yang. Happy hour is from 7pm to 8pm and there's live music most nights. (88/4 Th Hat Nai Yang; admission free; ☉11am-1am)

Top Experiences
Day-Trippin' Ko Phi-Phi

Getting There

Boats depart the Rassada pier at 9am, 2.30pm and 3pm and return from Phi-Phi at 9am, 1.30pm and 3pm (400B, two hours).

Plenty of tour companies also run day trips to Phi-Phi.

Curving bays, white-sand beaches and breathtaking rock formations that rise from the vivid turquoise waters – Ko Phi-Phi turns that tropical-island cliché into a stunning reality. Grab a long tail out to Ko Phi-Phi Leh to retrace the steps of Leo in the filming of *The Beach*, head underwater for some excellent diving, check out the stunning viewpoint or just kick back for the day. You deserve it!

Ko Phi-Phi Leh

Don't Miss

Diving & Snorkelling

It's not just the tourists that take a shine to this neck of the woods; abundant marine life gathers in the crystal-clear Andaman waters making it a top spot to strap on a mask and a pair of flippers.

Popular dive sites include the **King Cruiser Wreck**, sitting a mere 12m below the surface; **Anemone Reef**, teeming with hard corals and clownfish; **Hin Bida**, a submerged pinnacle attracting turtles; and **Ko Bida Nok**, with its signature karst massif luring leopard sharks. A two-dive trip with **Adventure Club** (☏08 1970 0314; www.phi-phi-adventures.com) starts from 2500B.

For snorkelling, flipper around Ko Mai Phai (Bamboo Island), 5km north of Phi-Phi Don (the main island) for a chance to see small sharks. Trips start from 800B. Another good spot for underwater delights is along the eastern coast of Ko Nok, near Ao Ton Sai, and along the eastern coast of Ko Nai.

The Viewpoint

If you can't make it to the surrounding islands, brave the sweaty climb to Phi-Phi's viewpoint to see what you're missing. It's about a 20 minute hike up the mountain path and at the top there are stunning views of the twin bays, craggy limestone formations and Ko Phi-Phi Leh.

Ko Phi-Phi Leh

Ever since Alex Garland's bestseller, *The Beach*, was made into a movie and filmed here, Ko Phi-Phi Leh has become somewhat of a pilgrimage site for backpackers. You can organise a long-tail boat here from Phi-Phi Don to swim and relax on its small sandy beaches.

☑ Top Tips

▸ Get to the Rassada pier early to ensure a good spot as the boats get crowded.

▸ If you've got the time, stay overnight to experience Phi-Phi's nightlife once the day-trippers leave.

▸ Tread lightly and clean up after yourself. Phi-Phi's fragile ecosystem and infrastructure struggles to cope with the influx of tourists it receives.

✕ Take a Break

Grab lunch at **Ciao Bella** (☏08 1894 1246; dishes 150B-300B; ◷breakfast, lunch & dinner) on the sand in Ao Lo Dalam, a perennial favourite for expats and travellers, where you can dine on fresh seafood and great pizzas in a romantic setting by the sea.

Top Experiences
Rock Climbing at Hat Railay, Krabi

Getting There

Boats leave Tha Bang Bong (north of Phuket's main pier, Th Rassada) to Krabi's Kha Khong pier. From here, a long-tail boat takes you to Railay (150B, 45 minutes). A further longtail boat (50B) takes you to Tham Phra Nang.

Surrounded by craggy limestone cliffs jutting out over emerald waters and sandy beaches, Krabi's Railay Peninsula is the ultimate jungle gym for rock climbers. With nearly 500 bolted routes, ranging from beginner to challenging advanced climbs, all with unparalleled clifftop vistas, this is among one of the top rock-climbing destinations in the world. And after scaling the limestone, hit the turquoise waters of Ao Nang, just a long-tail boat ride around the corner.

Don't Miss

The Climbs

Most climbers start at **Muay Thai Wall** and **One, Two, Three Wall**, at the southern end of Hat Railay East, which have at least 40 routes graded from 4b to 8b on the French system. The mighty **Thaiwand Wall** sits at the southern end of Hat Railay West and offers a sheer limestone cliff with some of the most challenging climbing routes. Other top climbs include **Hidden World** (for intermediate climbers), **Wee's Present Wall, Diamond Cave** and **Ao Nang Tower** (a three-pitch climbing wall reached only by long tail). **King Climbers** (☎0 7563 7125; www.railay.com), one of the most reputable schools, offers half-day climbs for 1000B and full-day for 1800B.

Tham Phra Nang

The claim to fame of Tham Phra Nang (Princess Cave) is that it's full of colourful wooden penises! It's actually an important shrine for local fishers, and legend has it that a royal barge carrying an Indian princess foundered in a storm here during the 3rd century. The spirit of the drowned princess came to inhabit the cave, granting favours to all who paid their respects. Local fishermen – Muslim and Buddhist – still place carved wooden phalluses in the cave as offerings in the hope that the spirit will provide plenty of fish. And what do schlongs have to do with anything? Some say because she died a virgin, and some say it'll help with fertility...

Ao Nang

After the serenity and peacefulness of Railay, things liven up substantially at tourist-oriented Ao Nang. Its golden sand beaches are magnets for travellers and its waters are lovely to explore by kayak or for snorkelling among colourful fish. It's a 15-minute boat ride from Railay (80B).

☑ Top Tips

▶ Tham Phra Nang is only accessible by long-tail boat, and is best visited in the morning to avoid the afternoon rush of day-trippers.

✕ Take a Break

For a caffeine hit before you tackle the rocks, **Highland Rock Climbing** (☎08 0693 0374; Hat Railay) has a cafe cobbled from driftwood and dangling with orchids, and the coffee beans are sourced from sustainable farms in Chiang Rai.

Top Experiences
Hidden Hongs of Ao PhangNga

Getting There

Best option is a day trip with a tour operator. Alternatively, catch a bus from Phuket to Phang-Nga (85B, 1½ hours). Tha Dan is 8.5km south of the town centre; you can charter boats from there.

With just the gentle lull of your kayak's paddle in the water, sit back and enjoy the tranquil confines of Ao PhangNga's famed *hongs* (lagoons enclosed by 360-degrees of limestone rock). It may be swarming with tourists in motorboats year-round, but once you enter, awe descends upon your group as you silently navigate its incredible scenery.

Getting out here is a big part of the fun, with a boat cruise taking you past dramatic limestone karsts soaring from the turquoise sea, lifted straight from the pages of glossy travel brochures.

Don't Miss

Hong by Starlight

Slip through pitch-black bat caves into a hidden lagoon protected by limestone cliffs that rise spectacularly from the sea. Along the way you'll be accompanied by sea eagles, and will most likely see monkeys and possibly pythons and monitor lizards, making the experience all the more exotic. **John Gray** (☑ 0 7625 4505-7; www.johngray-seacanoe. com; 124 Soi 1, Th Yaowarat) was the first kayak outfitter in the bay. His Hong by Starlight day trip dodges the crowds, involves plenty of sunset paddling (guided, not self-paddle) and you may see Ao PhangNga's famed bioluminescence once night falls (usually if there's been some rain).

Ao Phang-Nga Marine National Park

Covering an area of 400 sq km, Ao Phang-Nga Marine National Park is noted for its classic karst scenery, created by mainland fault movements that pushed massive limestone blocks into geometric patterns. As these blocks extended southward into Ao PhangNga, they formed more than 40 islands with huge vertical cliffs. The bay itself is composed of large and small tidal channels that originally connected with the mainland river system.

The Islands

The biggest tourist drawcard in the Ao Phang-Nga Marine National Park is the so-called 'James Bond Island', known to Thais as Ko Phing Kan (literally 'Leaning on Itself Island'). Once used as a location setting for *The Man with the Golden Gun*, the island is now full of vendors hawking coral and shells that should have stayed in the sea. For a more peaceful day, head to Ko Klui, which has tidal access to a huge *hong* and a pristine white-sand beach with plenty of hornbills and monkeys.

☑ **Top Tips**

► It's a long day on the water, so don't forget your hat, bathers, sunnies and sunscreen.

► It's easiest to join a sea-canoeing trip as a day tour from Phuket

✗ **Take a Break**

Most tours will include lunch. Otherwise dine overlooking the river at **Kror Son Thong**, south of the commercial strip of Phang-Nga town. This kitchen serves *pla tod kamin* (turmeric fried fish), crab omelette and roast duck with kale. It's all excellent.

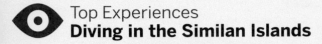

Top Experiences
Diving in the Similan Islands

Getting There

Day tours (day/night 3000/5000B) and live aboards (three days 14,500B) are the best way; or take a bus from Phuket Town to Khao Lak (two hours), and a boat (return 1700B, 1½ hours) from Taplamu pier.

A regular feature in Top 10 lists of the world's best sites, the Similan Islands Marine National Park is Thailand's premier dive spot. While it'll delight with its kaleidoscope of swaying soft corals, tropical fish, turtles and the occasional whale shark, it's perhaps better known for its underwater gorges and dramatic granite boulder swim-throughs. The archipelago comprises nine granite islands, which are as impressive above water as below, with their rainforest, blissful white beaches and gin-clear waters.

Don't Miss

Getting Under Water

The underwater landscapes on the western side of the Similans are a unique place to dive, with rocky drop-offs, granite boulders and a labyrinth of dive-throughs. The east coast is more of an explosion of colour, with its soft corals home to exotic marine life. The Similans offer diving for all levels of experience, at depths from 2m to 30m. There's good snorkelling too, and kids will love it, with coral reefs starting from the low-tide mark on **Ko Miang** (island 4) and **Ko Similan** (island 8). Recently, the park was expanded to include **Ko Bon** and **Ko Tachai**, and both have remained unscathed by coral bleaching, making them some of the better diving and snorkelling areas.

Wildlife & Hiking

Life's not all about getting under water here. The forest around the park headquarters on Ko Miang has walking trails and some great wildlife. The fabulous Nicobar pigeon, with its wild mane of grey-green feathers, is common here. Endemic to the islands of the Andaman Sea, it's one of some 39 bird species in the park. Hairy-legged land crabs and fruit bats are relatively easily seen in the forest, as are flying squirrels.

Detouring from the track, the **Viewpoint Trail** – 500m or so of steep scrambling – has panoramic vistas from the top. A 500m walk to **Sunset Point** takes you through forest to a smooth granite platform facing west. On Ko Similan there's a 2.5km forest hike to a viewpoint, and a shorter, steep scramble off the main beach to the top of **Sail Rock** (aka Balance Rock).

www.dnp.go.th

admission 400B

⊙ Nov-May

☑ Top Tips

▶ The Similans are closed from 1 May to 1 November.

▶ Diving is always good, but February to April has the best visibility.

▶ Organised tours from Phuket are the way to go, costing little more than you'd pay trying to get to the islands independently.

✕ Take a Break

The **restaurant** (dishes 100-150B) on island 4 serves simple Thai meals, but food's generally included on tour packages.

JEFF HUNTER/GETTY IMAGES ©

The Best of
Phuket

Phuket's Best Walks

Phuket's Best...

Wat Chalong (p79)
WIBOWO RUSLI/GETTY IMAGES ©

Best Walks
Phuket Town's Architectural Legacies

🏃 The Walk

On an island that attracts millions of beach goers every year, it's easy to overlook Phuket Town with its lack of white sand and blue waters. However, this is precisely the reason you should visit! The town offers a rare insight into the history of Phuket and this walk through the Old Town will take you past the architectural legacies of the Baba people.

Start Standard Chartered Bank

Finish Phuket Thaihua Museum

Length 1km; 1½ hours

✖ Take a Break

On Th Thalang, just before you reach China Inn, **Wilai** (📞 0 7622 2875; 14 Th Thalang; dishes from 65B; 🕙 10am-4pm, closed Sun) serves fantastic Phuket soul food.

Phuket Thaihua Museum

LYNN GAIL/GETTY IMAGES ©

❶ Standard Chartered Bank

Start at the intersection of Th Phang Nga and Th Thepkasatri where you'll find the Standard Chartered Bank built in classic Sino-Portuguese style. This was the first local bank in Thailand, and is now a museum showcasing Phuket's Baba history.

❷ Police Station

Opposite is the Thai police building, which was built to protect the bank in the early 1900s. It has a unique four-storey clock tower with traditional police-cap roof. The clock-tower face stood blank for 50 years until there was the budget for a clock.

❸ Post Office/ Philatetic Museum

Head east along Th Phang Nga, taking note of cafes and restaurants in beautiful old shop-houses. Turn left onto Th Montri and you'll see the old post office building, a magnificent example of Phuket's Sino-Portuguese architecture, which now houses the Phuket Philatelic Museum.

❹ China Inn

Continue north along Th Montri, turn left at Th Thalang and wander this historic street full of converted shophouses. Pass Soi Romanee, a gorgeous street worth exploring at night. China Inn is a short walk to your left; more than 100 years old, the restored building is a classic Chinese shophouse with beautiful detailing.

❺ Thanon Dibuk

Follow Th Thalang west until Th Yaowarat, turn right and walk a few minutes until Th Dibuk and turn left. Wide Th Dibuk has some fine Sino-Portuguese shophouses with elegant facades.

❻ Blue Elephant

At the T intersection at the end of Th Dibuk, turn left. Follow Th Satun to the end where it meets Th Krabi and explore the gardens on the corner. The former Phra Pitak Chinpracha Mansion building here has been immaculately restored and converted into Phuket's finest dining establishment.

❼ Chinpracha House

Next to Blue Elephant, a gravel path leads to Chinpracha House. Built in 1903 by Prapitak Chinpracha, it now houses a private museum.

❽ Phuket Thaihua Museum

Head back past Blue Elephant, continuing east along Th Krabi to Phuket Thaihua Museum. Built in 1934, this was the oldest Chinese school in Thailand; it exhibits a top mix of European-Sino-Thai architectural styles.

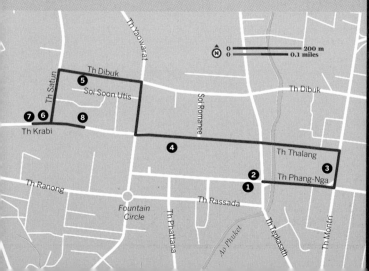

Best
Beaches

Ninety-nine percent of visitors to Phuket are heading straight for the beach – and no wonder why. No matter what your beach requirements, Phuket has it covered. White sand and clear blue waters lap along the 45km stretch of coast, where flashy developed strands alternate with secret castaway paradises.

So Which Is for You?

It's the west-coast beaches that lure 5.3 million tourists here annually. From the earthy, rocky coves on the south coast to that wide web of lust that is pulsing Patong, to the gorgeous yet discreet north, Phuket's coastline contorts and twists into various shapes and sizes, giving each stretch of sand its own rhythm.

The majority of visitors are attracted to the entrenched tourist magnets of Kata and Karon, and, of course, Patong. If you're after a social scene, this is where you come – long stretches of sand lined with resorts, restaurants, bars and other facilities you might need just steps away. On most beaches you'll find sun loungers for rent and water sports to keep you busy – from banana boats and surfboards to jet skis and parasailing. If you prefer a more peaceful, secluded vibe, you'll find it in rocky coves, off nondescript coastal roads, over boulders and through tunnels in-between the main beaches and on Phuket's northern coast.

For Families

Hat Kata A pleasant half-moon crescent bay ideal for families with good swimming and facilities. (p62)

Hat Karon Popular for its long, wide stretch of sand and space to spread out. (p62)

Hat Nai Han Nestled at the southern tip of the island, it has a quiet local feel. (p77)

Hat Kamala Calm waters and good snorkelling at its northern end. (p88)

Hidden Spots

Freedom Beach A longtail boat ride away from the madness of Patong. (p44)

Hat Mai Khao

Hat Ya Nui A laid-back sandy beach cove backed by lush mountains. (p77)

Ao Sane This tucked-away secret has a small white sand beach amid boulders. (p79)

Laem Singh A beautiful cape walled in by cliffs and no road access. (p87)

Water Activities

Hat Patong You name it, it's here. Parasailing, jet skis and loads more. (p44)

Hat Kata Great for surfing and snorkelling, particularly at Kata Noi. (p62)

Hat Kamala Decent surf breaks and parasailing, and great for a spot of snorkelling. (p88)

Hat Nai Yang A good choice for snorkelling in the dry season and for surfing in the monsoon. (p109)

Long Walks

Hat Mai Khao Phuket's longest beach, where you can walk for hours in isolation. (p109)

Hat Karon This squeaky white-sand stretch goes on for miles and is perfect for stretching the legs. (p62)

Ao Bang Thao A beautiful 8km sweep of white sand and a relaxed feel. (p97)

Relaxation

Hat Surin Stylish, yet unpretentious, Surin retains a laid-back village feel. (p87)

Hat Mai Khao Most of the time you'll be lucky enough to have this one all to yourself. (p109)

Hat Nai Thon A quiet, peaceful beach with not too many distractions. (p109)

Hat Kamala With its rustic, mellow feel, Kamala is perfect for relaxing. (p88)

Best
Dining

PETER WIDMANN/ALAMY ©

Beachfront dining, bamboo shacks, street food and high-end resorts: Phuket makes for some seriously good eating. No matter where you do it, eating will be a big part of your Phuket holiday. All budgets and tastes are catered for, from locally caught fresh seafood and seven-course degustation menus to spicy local arse-burning dishes and home-style Western comfort food.

High-End Dining

Most of the island's high-end dining is in the glitzy resorts lining the coast, particularly in Kata. There are a number of ultracool and classy spots on the hill overlooking Kalim Bay near Patong, and a recent fad of beach clubs popping up all over the place has also brought some more excellent dining and gourmet food with it. But for anyone wanting to sample some of Phuket's best food at more affordable prices, a night dining out in Phuket Town is a must.

Local Eats

To sample some of Phuket's best local restaurants, you'll need to head to Phuket Town once you're done feasting on the seafood grills around the beaches. The Old Town has a number of generations-old eateries housed in character-filled Sino-Portuguese buildings serving classic Thai and Phuketian fare.

Beachfront

The Catch Indulge in a gourmet buffet at this classy beach club. (p89)

Boathouse Wine & Grill Sea breezes and upmarket dining at Phuket's most reputable restaurant on Hat Kata. (p65)

Rockfish Sophisticated beach shack perched on the rocky end of Hat Kamala. (p90)

Mom Tri's Kitchen Stunning Kata Noi views and fusion haute cuisine. (p65)

Taste The best of a new breed of urban-meets-surf eateries along the beach. (p89)

Coconut Tree Dine with the sand between your toes at this relaxed spot. (p113)

Baan Rim Pa

Special Night Out

Blue Elephant The finest addition to Phuket's culinary credentials, set in a stunning Sino-Portuguese mansion. (p29)

9th Floor A diamond among the rough in Patong with city and sea views. (p46)

Baan Rim Pa Candlelight, soft piano tunes and traditional Thai. (p46)

Seafood

Patcharin Local open-air seafood shack on the headland at Hat Surin. (p91)

Baan Rimlay Fresh steamed seafood and a superb location in Rawai. (p80)

Savoey One of the best seafood grills on the island, with fresh lobster. (p48)

Batik Specialises in grilled fish, fresh from the market. (p111)

Bella Vista Perched above Ska Bar, this Swiss-run restaurant shares the same beautiful banyan tree and stunning sea views. (p65)

Inexpensive Thai

Raya A perennial favourite of locals, set in a Sino-Portuguese building. (p31)

The Orchids Well known for its classic Thai dishes, just steps from Hat Patong. (p47)

Oyjoi Number 1 Delightful garden cafe popular

for its excellent cheap Thai food. (p81)

Pad Thai Shop Keeping it real in Kata, a no-frills spot famous for its *pàt tai*. (p68)

The Cook Sensational, inexpensive Italian–Thai fusion. (p31)

Andaman Dine on BBQ seafood and Thai curries right by the water's edge. (p97)

Chao Lay Bistro Tasty Thai food in a hip, open-air dining room. (p111)

Healthy

Living Food Cafe It's not all gluttony here; this cafe serves interesting raw-food dishes. (p82)

Naughty Radish Detox juices and salads offer a break from cocktails and curries. (p47)

Best
Spas & Massage

Once you're done partying and paddling, it's time for some pampering. Scrub, massage, wrap and rub your way to comatose beach bliss at any number of spas and massage joints across the island. Splurge or save depending on your needs. Brave a muscle-pounding Thai massage or opt for a soothing body scrub and relaxing steam bath – the choices are endless.

Choosing Your Spa

There seems to be a massage shop on every corner on Phuket. Most are low-key family affairs where traditional Thai massage goes for about 250B per hour, and a basic mani-pedi costs around 150B – a real steal. The quality of service at these places varies, and changes rapidly as staff turnover is high. Go with your gut instinct or ask fellow travellers or your hotel staff for recommendations. No matter where you choose, it's still a massage and is likely to be extremely pleasant and relaxing.

If you're looking for a more Western spa experience, head to one of Phuket's plentiful spa resorts. These places are often affiliated with a ritzy hotel (but nearly all are open to nonguests). They are haute couture affairs with sumptuous Zen designs and huge treatment menus.

Best Indulgence

The Spa At Karon's Mövenpick resort, this is the one of the most atmospheric spas in the area. (p63)

Sala Resort & Spa Treat yourself to a beachfront massage at this hip and sexy resort. (p109)

Spa Royale Seaside treatment rooms and highly trained therapists at Mom Tri's Villa Royale. (p63)

Coqoon Spa Stunning rainforest surrounds and five-star treatment in Hat Nai Yang. (p110)

LONELY PLANET/GETTY IMAGES ©

Beachfront massage, Hat Kata

Best for Couples

Palm Spa Book the VIP room for couples, featuring a rose petal bath. (p88)

Sala Couples' rooms are slick and spacious with aromatic milky baths in a private pebbled courtyard. (p109)

Swasana You'll be nested in a glass cube on cushy mats together at the end of Hat Patong. (p44)

Aspasia Hidden away at a seaside condo resort on the headland between Kata and Karon. (p64)

Best for Less

Mandarin Massage Cheap, clean and cheerful on Surin's main drag, with an aloe vera massage. (p89)

First Foot Relax 2 Upmarket dark-wood interior with reasonably priced indulgent treatments. (p45)

The Raintree Spa A great-value Phuket Town spa in tranquil garden surrounds. (p28)

Let's Relax A haven from Patong's busy streets, with a range of affordable treatments. (p44)

The Real Deal

Atsumi Healing A wellness and detox centre with deep-tissue and oil massage treatments. (p78)

Waree Spa A local spa with a proper Scandinavian sauna for sweating our those toxins. (p110)

Best
For Romance

You'll spot loved-up couples everywhere in Phuket. When they're not strolling along the beach or indulging in couples' massages, they're feeding each other fresh seafood at beachfront restaurants and snuggling together in dimly lit bars. Who can blame them, when Phuket dishes up romantic options time and time again? Here are some of the island's best ways to spend your days with your loved one.

Beaches
You'll find some of Phuket's most pristine beaches in the north, with long stretches of white sand devoid of buzzing jet skis or hordes of beach goers – perfect for long romantic walks. The southern beaches offer more action, with beachfront bars and restaurants for intimate nights out. Phuket's craggy coastline offers some incredible viewpoints to cuddle up with your better half while watching the flame-red sun set into the Andaman Sea.

Spas
You'll find hip and sexy day spas all over the island where you can pamper and preen together. Couples are well catered for in most places; you can indulge in aromatic baths, massages and treatments in private rooms. Otherwise some day spas offer the choice of private beachfront massages.

Beach Clubs
Exclusive beach clubs are a growing trend in Phuket. They provide the perfect excuse to laze around beachside infinity pools or on deckchairs, dine on gourmet cuisine, drink cocktails, and swim all day while being waited on hand and foot.

M SOBREIRA/ALAMY ©

Restaurants

Baan Rim Pa Plenty of candlelight and sea views at this upmarket Thai winner. (p46)

Boathouse Phuket's classic 'special night out' spot with red roses, beachside dining and a long wine list to enjoy. (p65)

Rockfish Perched on the rocky end of Kamala beach, the perfect hideaway for two. (p90)

Viewpoints

Laem Phromthep
Cosy up to your loved one, while watching the fireball sunset drop into the Andaman Sea, at the island's famous viewpoint. (p74)

Hat Mai Khao

Khao Rang Get a bird's-eye view of Phuket Town while leisurely lunching at one of the romantic spots up here. (p27)

Secret View Point Escape the crowds here to watch the sunset in peace. (p77)

Intimate Bars

White Box Toast the two of you in style overlooking Kalim Bay. (p50)

Sanaeha Sip classy cocktails in the dimly lit corners of Phuket Town's coolest bar. (p33)

On the Rocks Sink your toes into the sand at this rustic shack among the rocks at Kata Beach. (p69)

Spas

Palm Spa Check into the VIP room for a rose-petal bath for two. (p88)

Sala You'll feel like celebrities as you indulge at this hip and sexy spa. (p109)

The Spa Let your stresses float away with the 2½ hour couples' massage at the Mövenpick's ambient spa. (p63)

Beach Walks

Ao Bang Thao Take a sunset stroll hand-in-hand along this stunning stretch of white-sand beach. (p97)

Hat Mai Khao Walk for hours without seeing another soul on Phuket's longest beach. (p109)

Hat Nai Thon Get away from the crowds at this beautiful arc of golden sand and stroll to the headland. (p109)

Activities

John Gray's Seacanoe Float through hidden peaceful lagoons on a twilight kayak trip to Ao PhangNga. (p119)

Phuket Heritage Trails Take a guided tour of the Old Town's beautiful Sino-Portuguese mansions. (p27)

Ko Phi-Phi Re-enact a scene from *The Beach* (the love scene, not Leo's bizarre drug delirium) on a day trip. (p114)

Best
Ways to Party

Phuket ain't no wallflower, and most visitors come here well up-to-speed on that. Beachside drinking shacks, hip bars, pulsing nightclubs and Patong's carnival of sin is what lures most people in. And it's not all about cheap shots and go-go bars when you've got some of the hottest clubs, boxing and grandiose theatrical performances here.

Clubs

Seduction One of Patong's hottest clubs with occasional global DJs, and slick lighting and design. (p50)

Liquid Lounge A cool cocktail lounge with occasional live jazz in a stylish loft. (p92)

Factory Bar Factory has a huge dancefloor and couches, overlooking all the action of Bangla. (p51)

Laid-Back Bars

Rick 'n' Roll Music Bar A great place to meet other travellers over a cold beer and live music. (p69)

Mr Pan's Mini Art Space This quirky bar mixes drinks and art, with an attached studio. (p69)

Skyla's Beach House Perched at the end of Kamala beach is this rustic beach-shack bar. (p92)

Bars to be Seen

Sanaeha The hippest bar in town has several spots to hang out with a classy cocktail. (p33)

White Box Oozing sex appeal at the rocky end of Kalim Bay is the ultramodern White Box. (p50)

Beach Club Bar A chic outdoor beachside lounge at the Catch Beach Club in Surin. (p92)

Entertainment

Phuket Simon Cabaret This theatrical ladyboy show is the quintessential Patong experience. (p51)

Phuket Pub Crawl Head to Bangla for the ultimate debauched night out in Patong. (p40)

Bangla Boxing Stadium Watch competitors battle it out with *moo•ay tai* (Thai boxing; also *muay thai*) bouts. (p52)

Beachside Bars

Ska Bar A great bar tucked into the rocks at the southern end of Hat Kata. (p69)

Royal Phuket Yacht Club Drink in style on the decking overlooking all of Patong bay. (p82)

Nikita's Feel the sea breeze here at Rawai's beach, with a drink in hand and the sand between your toes. (p82)

On the Rocks A rustic shack on the sand at the end of Kata Noi. (p69)

Best
Ways to Cure a Hangover

Beach holidays are synonymous with cocktails and, well, more cocktails. You start late afternoon, have some more cocktails at dinner and before you know it, you're in Th Bangla or some random bar at 2am in the morning before a groggy stumble back to your resort. Maybe one more vodka at the hotel bar... The next morning, the sun is shining, but this time it hurts, and you're in need of a good hangover cure. It might be a greasy fry-up, a healthy juice, a snooze on the beach or good old 'hair of the dog' that gets you back on track.

BOBI/GETTY IMAGES ©

Breakfasts

Gallery Cafe Number one spot for a big brekky after bar-hopping in Phuket Town. (p32)

Naughty Radish Grab a detox juice and a healthy start to the day before hitting Patong Beach. (p47)

Live Present Moment Sleep in and then head here for the all-day breakfast in Kamala. (p89)

Beach Clubs

Catch Beach Club Lounge around on plush daybeds looking out to Hat Surin. (p87)

Bliss Beach Club Soak up the five-star service. You won't need to lift a finger for food, drink or stunning views. (p97)

Re Ká Ta Relax in the infinity pool or lie around under your umbrella at this exclusive beach club. (p63)

Coffee

Monkeypod Stop off for the best coffee on the island on the way the gibbons and a waterfall walk. (p105)

Eco Cafe Sip your organic latte while gazing out to Phuket Town's architecture in your hungover daze. (p34)

Italian Job Pep up with a classic espresso before a long walk along Kata Beach. (p70)

Daytime Bars

After Beach Bar Go the 'hair of the dog' philosophy and cure your hangover with a cold frothy and spectacular Kata views. (p68)

On the Rocks Let the sea breezes clear your head at this quiet spot at Kata Noi. (p69)

Ska Bar Look out over Kata and ease away the pain with beers and Rasta tunes. (p69)

Activities

Kata Hot Yoga A sure-fire hangover cure is to sweat it all out, and hot yoga will guarantee that. (p64)

Khao Phra Thaew National Park Get back to nature on a waterfall walk. (p103)

Best
Diving &
Snorkelling

Phuket enjoys an enviable central location relative to the Andaman's top diving destinations. The much-talked-about Similan Islands sit to the north, while dozens of dive sites surround nearby Ko Phi-Phi and Ko Lanta to the south. Most operators on Phuket take divers to Ko Raya Noi and Ko Raya Yai (also called Racha Noi and Racha Yai), where you can see soft corals and pelagic fish species aplenty. Manta rays are also frequently glimpsed around here and, if you're lucky, even whale sharks. The best diving months are December to May. There's fantastic snorkelling at most of the surrounding islands, particulalry the Similans, and there's some good marine life at the beaches of Kata, Hat Nai Thon and Laem Singh.

REINHARD DIRSCHERL/GETTY IMAGES ©

Patong

Scuba Cat Live-aboard dive and kayak trips to the Similan and Surin Islands. Discover Scuba course for uncertified beginners and plenty of day trips on offer. Has been around for 20 years and gets rave reviews. A new branch has opened up in Kee Plaza. (www.scubacat.com; 78/19 Thawiwong)

Kon-Tiki Opposite the Novotel, this Scandinavian-run dive shop has been in the business for more than 30 years and has instructors who speak English, German, Danish, Swedish and Norwegian. They mix a bit of diving with relaxing, hosting sunset BBQs on the boat. Also has outlets in Karon and Mai Khao. (www.kontiki -thailand.com, 120/1-3 Th Rat Uthit)

Kata & Karon

Dive Asia Dive Asia hits the usual southern-reef day trips, teaches a full curriculum of classes, and has live-aboard options to the Similan and Surin Islands. Also sells snorkels and masks.(www.diveasia. com; 24 Th Karon, Hat Kata)

Sunrise Divers Managed by Phuket blogger Jamie Monk, this is the biggest live-aboard agent in Phuket and can arrange a variety of trips from Similan Islands boat trips to backpacker grunge to sweet luxury from a comprehensive listing of dive companies. (www. sunrise-divers.com; 269/24 Th Patak East, Hat Karon)

Best
Cultural
Experiences

While it can be hard to tear yourself away from slothing about on the beach, just try, as there are some well-worthy sights and activities to explore on land to connect you with the destination you're holidaying in. Phuket Town is the cultural heart of the island but each area has a local experience on offer.

M SOBREIRA/ALAMY ©

Museums

Thalang National Museum Chronicles Phuket's history and traces the various ethnicities found in southern Thailand. (p103)

Chinpracha House This Sino-Portuguese mansion turned museum is one for antiques lovers. (p27; interior pictured above)

Phuket Thaihua Museum Filled with photos and exhibits on Phuket's Chinese and tin-mining history. (p27)

Cooking Classes

Blue Elephant Cooking School Master Thai speciality recipes in a restored Sino-Portuguese mansion. (p27)

Boathouse Cooking Class Phuket's most popular cooking classes where you learn to make five dishes. (p62)

Temples & Shrines

Big Buddha Still under construction but almost complete, this will be one of the largest Buddha statues on earth. (p58)

Shrine of the Serene Light Check out the Taoist etchings and vaulted ceilings at this evocative shrine. (p25)

Wat Chalong This temple possesses a spiritual vibration, especially when worshippers pay their respects. (p79)

Wat Phra Thong Phuket's 'Temple of the Gold Buddha' is half buried, so that only the head and shoulders are visible above ground. (p103)

Best
For Kids

Eateries

Crepes Village They'll love these sweet or savoury crepes in a fairy-lit garden. (p80)

Da Vinci Kids get a playground while parents get some peace at this open-air Italian spot. (p80)

Bocconcino Creamy gelato served in cup or cone in this bright, cheery cafe. (p91)

Theme Parks

Dino Park Minigolf with a maze of caves, lagoons, leafy gardens and dinosaur statues. (p64)

Splash Jungle Some seriously cool waterslides here just perfect for kids bored with the beach. (p110)

Animal Action

Butterfly Garden & Insect World A world of creepy crawlies inside and butterfly fun outside. (p28)

Phuket Aquarium Loads of underwater delights here including sharks and an electric eel. (p29)

Feed the Monkeys Head out to this bizarre sight where hundreds of Macaques come for a feed. (p29)

Phuket Gibbon Rehabilitation Centre This tiny sanctuary adopts gibbons that have been kept in captivity in the hope they can be reintroduced to the wild. (p103)

BRENT MADISON/GETTY IMAGES ©

Activities

Phuket Fantasea An over-the-top extravaganza of acrobats, performing elephants and Thai dance. (p88)

Kok Chang Safari Take an elephant ride up the mountain at this well-run camp. (p63)

Phuket Riding Club Trot through the jungle or along the beach on horseback. (p79)

Best
Water Activities

Water activities abound in Phuket, which isn't surprising considering it is an island! The Andaman Sea is a travellers' playground where you can head underwater to discover a kaleidoscope of marine life while diving or snorkelling, sail high above on a parasail or flit about its surface on a surfboard, kiteboard or jet ski. Surfing and kiteboarding are fast becoming two of the more popular pursuits.

PAUL KENNEDY/GETTY IMAGES ©

Surfing

Phuket is one of Thailand's premier surf destinations. Once the monsoons bring their mid-year swell, glassy seas fold into barrels. The best waves arrive between June and September. Kata, at the south end of the bay, is near one of the best breaks, which typically tops out at 2m. Hat Nai Han can get bigger waves (up to 3m) near the yacht club. Be warned: both Kata and Nai Han have vicious undertows that can claim lives. Kalim is sheltered and has a consistent break that also gets up to 3m. This is a hollow wave, and is considered the best break on the island. Kamala's northernmost beach has a nice gentle beach break and Hat Nai Yang has a consistent, if soft, wave that breaks more than 200m off shore.

Kiteboarding

One of the world's fastest growing sports is also one of Phuket's latest fads. The two best spots are Hat Nai Yang (May to late-October) and Rawai (November to February). Most kiteboarding outfitters are affiliated with the International Kiteboarding Organization (think PADI for kites).

Surfing

Phuket Surf Offers surf lessons and board rental in Hat Kata. (p64)

Skyla's Beach House A great source of surfing info with lessons and board rental in Kamala. (p88)

Praphat Sea Sports Club Surf lessons and board hire in Patong. (p46)

Kiteboarding

Kite Zone Has courses ranging in length from an hour to five days. (p79)

Kiteboarding Asia Main office is on Hat Nai Yang; also offers lessons off Rawai's Friendship Beach. (www.kiteboarding asia.com)

Best
For a Rainy Day

While we all pray for sunny skies when we book that beach holiday, the reality is that in tropical paradises such as Phuket, sudden downpours can drown you without warning and have you scuttling from the beach before twiddling your thumbs about what to do next. Fortunately, Phuket knows this and has plenty of wet-weather options.

FELIX HUG/GETTY IMAGES ©

Shopping

Jung Ceylon Sure it's a shopping mall but it has plenty of ways to spend your cash on a rainy day. (p54)

Lemongrass House Gorgeous store selling a range of all-natural health and beauty products. (p93)

Ban Boran Textiles Great for raw silk, jewellery and linen clothes. (p35)

Parin Waris Sells an interesting range of homemade organic beauty products. (p70)

Spas

Let's Relax Indulge indoors with gushing fountains and soothing massages. (p44)

The Spa While it's wet outside, you can indulge in a body scrub in your seaside room. (p63)

Coqoon Spa With these rainforest surrounds, the rain will only make your massage better. (p110)

Cooking Classes

Pum Thai Cooking School Things will heat up as you cook fiery curries at Pum Thai. (p45)

Blue Elephant Cooking School You'll hardly notice the rain in this massive cooking-school mansion. (p27)

Boathouse Cooking Class Stay dry while learning culinary secrets from one of the best on the island. (p62)

Museums

Thalang National Museum Wait it out as you bone up on Phuket's history at this interesting museum. (p103)

Phuket Thaihua Museum This flashy museum has plenty of displays and exhibits to while away the day. (p27)

Best
Guys' Getaway

Adventure

Nicky's Handlebar Joy-ride on a Harley or take a Ferrari for a lap around Patong. (p44)

Cable Jungle Adventure Zip-line 100m through the lush jungles of Thalang. (p104)

Jungle Bungy Jump Bungy from 20 stories up or get shot high into the air on the Rocket Man jump. (p46)

Bars & Clubs

Rockin' Angels Chug cheap beer and listen to rockin' tunes in Phuket Town. (p33)

Rick 'n' Roll Music Cafe Meet other travellers at this casual bamboo bar with live music and BBQs. (p69)

Laguna Nightclub Party into the wee hours at this complex that has several bars to choose from. (p83)

Entertainment

Pub Crawl Patong Hit Th Bangla on a pub-and-grub crawl through the heart of Patong. (p40)

Phuket Shooting Range Choose from shooting, go-karting and paintball at this complex in Rawai. (p78)

AKHENATON LICHTEROWICZ/GETTY IMAGES ©

Bangla Boxing Stadium Witness *moo•ay tai* boxers go head-to-head in Patong. (p52)

Best
Girls' Getaway

Pampering

The Spa Absolute luxury indulgence at the most ambient spa in town. (p63)

Coqoon Spa Treat yourself to a frangipani body scrub in five-star surrounds. (p110)

Palm Spa Relax with a range of treatments at this decadent spa in Surin. (p88)

Shopping

Lemongrass House All-natural beauty products, scented soaps and body lotion. (p93)

Ban Boran Textiles Stock up on linen clothing and jewellery to take back home. (p35)

Island Paradise Chic boutique with stylishly flowing dresses and good handbags. (p36)

Beach Clubs

Re Ká Ta Laze around on plush furniture with cocktail in hand on Hat Kata. (p63)

Up Beach Club Exclusive club high on the hill overlooking the beach. (p109)

Catch Beach Club Sprawl out on your day bed under an umbrella with a bottle of bubbly. (p87)

Bars

Sanaeha Stylish bar in Phuket Town perfect for a girls' night out. (p33)

After Beach Bar Take in the stunning views while knocking back cheap drinks at this bamboo bar. (p68)

MICHAEL SNELL/GETTY IMAGES ©

Activities

Phuket Riding Club Choose between a horse ride along the beach or through the jungle. (p79)

Blue Elephant Cooking School One of the best restaurants on the island shows you their secrets. (p27)

Amazing Bike Tours Take a half-day bicycle tour through the pristine Khao Phra Thaew National Park. (p104)

Survival Guide

Survival Guide

Before You Go

Book Your Stay

☑ **Top Tip** During high season it can be impossible to find a room, so book well in advance during the Christmas/New Year period.

➡ Phuket is generally pricier compared to the rest of Thailand.

➡ Prices here are determined by seasons; the 'rainy' season sees rates drop by 40% to 60%.

➡ There are dozens of places to sleep in Phuket, from no-frills boxy rooms to stylish self-catering apartments, zenned-out holiday homes and countless five-star resorts.

➡ When choosing where you stay, you'll need to work out whether you want to be in the heart of the pumping nightlife of Patong; somewhere you can escape yet be close enough to make trips into town, like Kata or Karon; or somewhere far away from it all like the northern beaches.

When to Go

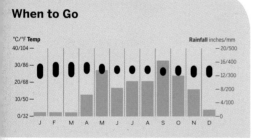

°C/°F **Temp**
40/104 —
30/86 —
20/68 —
10/50 —
0/32 —
J F M A M J J A S O N D

Rainfall inches/mm
— 20/500
— 16/400
— 12/300
— 8/200
— 4/100
—0

➡ **Rainy Season (May–Oct)** Chance your luck with the weather; plenty of sunshine mixed in with brief downpours, and the benefit of slashed prices and less crowds.

➡ **Peak Season (Dec–Jan)** Blue skies, and prices soar. All accommodation, fancy restaurants and transport need to be booked in advance.

➡ **Shoulder Season (mid-Jan–Mar)** Still has crowds, but not peak prices and weather is a good bet with calm waters.

Useful Websites

Agoda (www.agoda.com) Good deals on midrange hotels and resorts.

Phuket Hotels (www.phuket.com) Online booking and good info on the island.

Phuket Hotels & Travel Guide (www.phukethotels.com) Online booking site specialising in Phuket.

Wotif (www.wotif.com) Reliable online accommodation booking service.

Lonely Planet (www.lonelyplanet.com/phuket) Traveller forum and listings.

Best Budget

☑ **Top Tip** It's getting pretty difficult to find anything in Patong under 1000B between November and April, but Phuket Town is a treasure trove of budget lodging.

Patong Backpacker Hostel (www.phuketbackpacker.com) Great location near Hat Patong and its bars, with quality, good-value dorms.

Casa Jip (www.casajip.com) Italian run and great value for Patong, with big, if simple, rooms, comfy beds and a taste of Thai style.

Ao Sane Bungalows (☎ 0 7628 8306) Rickety wooden bungalows on a secluded Rawai beach, with million-dollar views and an old-hippy vibe.

Fantasy Hill Bungalow (fantasyhill@hotmail.com) Sitting in a lush garden on a hill, these Kata bungalows are peaceful but central.

Rick's Rock 'N' Roll (www.rnrhostel.com) Flying the flag for backpackers in Kata, Rick's is a good cheapie that balances laid-back with party central.

99 Old Town Boutique Guesthouse (99oldtown@hotmail.co.th) Atmospheric Phuket Town shophouse-turned-B&B.

Best Midrange

Caffe@Caffe (www.caffeatcaffe.com) Tiled rooms with gold wallpaper, striped duvets, mini-balconies, fridges and TVs make it as comfy as it is hip.

In On the Beach (www.karon-inonthebeach.com) A sweet, tasteful inn on Karon Park where rooms horseshoe the pool and come with sea views.

Baipho (www.baipho.com) Outrageously arty Patong guesthouse filled with Buddha imagery, modern art and urban touches.

Baan Pronphateep (www.baanpronphateep.com) Banyan-tree-shaded and nestled down a secluded little street is this quiet and simple three-star Patong choice.

ClearHouse (www.clearhousephuket.com) Shabby chic with a mod twist in Kamala. This place just feels good.

Benyada Lodge (www.benyadalodge-phuket.com) Modern rooms in Surin with a pool on the rooftop, just a short walk to the beach.

Best Top End

Evason Phuket Resort (www.sixsenses.com) Spa-hotel extraordinaire offers a copious amount of luxury, and encompasses private Bon Island.

Mom Tri's Villa Royale (www.villaroyalephuket.com) Supremely romantic place in a secluded Kata Noi location with beautiful rooms and the grandest of views.

Layalina Hotel (www.layalinahotel.com) Very private rooftop terraces with romantic sunset views over white sand and blue sea.

Mövenpick (www.moevenpick-hotels.com) Grab a secluded villa and choose from a private plunge pool or outdoor rainforest shower. Great for kids.

Surin Phuket (www.thesurinphuket.com) On a stunning private beach, bungalows with naturalistic wooden exteriors and luxurious interiors.

Banyan Tree Phuket (www.banyantree.com) An oasis of sedate, understated luxury. Bungalows have private pools.

Arriving in Phuket

Phuket International Airport

☑ **Top Tip** To escape Phuket's 'taxi mafia' (an organisation of overpriced chartered cars and túk-túks), get the phone number of a metered taxi and use the same driver throughout your stay in Phuket.

The vast majority of visitors will arrive at **Phuket International Airport** (www.phuketairportonline.com) either direct from international flights or via Bangkok. To get to the southern beaches, where most people stay, takes around 45 minutes to an hour.

Private taxi Easiest option to get to your hotel, costing 500B to 900B depending on your destination.

Metered taxis Located 50m to the right as you exit the arrivals hall, but you'll need to persuade them to use the meter, which works out to be 100B to 200B cheaper compared to private taxis.

Bus (www.airportbusphuket) Only serves Phuket Town (90B, 30 minutes), so not an option if you're staying at the beach.

Hire car Very convenient way to get around the island, and if you plan on hiring a car, you might as well start from the airport. **Avis** (☎ 08 9969 8674) and **Hertz** (☎ 0 2266 4666) have offices here. Prices start from 1500B per day.

Arriving by Boat

Phuket's Th Rassada, north of Phuket Town, is the main pier for boats to Ko Phi-Phi connecting onward to Krabi, Ko Lanta, the Trang Islands, Ko Lipe and even as far as Langkawi Island in Malaysia. For quicker service to Krabi and Ao Nang via the Ko Yao Islands, boats leave from Th Bang Bong north of Th Rassada.

Arriving by Bus & Minibus

If coming overland from Bangkok, you'll arrive at the **bus terminal** (☎ 0 7621 1977) in Phuket Town. Otherwise if you're on an air-con minibus, you'll likely be dropped at one of the main beaches.

Getting Around

Local Phuket transport is terrible. The systems in place make tourists either stay on their chosen beach, rent a car or motorbike (which can be hazardous) or take overpriced private car 'taxis' or túk-túks.

Private Taxi

Best for... Those who are not wanting to sign up for a day tour, yet want the freedom without self-drive.

➡ Air-conditioned car and driver costs about 1500B for eight hours.

➡ This option makes sense for those in a group, who can split the cost, making it an even better way of getting around.

Sŏrngtăaou (Passenger Pick-Up Trucks)

Best for... Budget travellers, and those who like to keep it local.

➡ These open-air buses run to all the beaches from Phuket Town, but the catch is that you'll have to go via Phuket Town to get from one beach to another (say Hat Surin to Hat Patong), which can take hours.

➡ Expect to pay around 30B per trip.

Túk-Túk

Best for... Getting from one beach to another, or short trips within town.

➡ Not the three-wheeler túk-túks you'll find elsewhere in Thailand, these red open-air vans are based in all towns.

➡ Used for local trips; also a popular but pricey way to get between beaches.

➡ Costs anywhere from 50B to 100B for shorter trips within a town, 200B to get from Kata to Karon, or 500B for longer journeys (eg Karon to Patong). Bargain hard, but don't expect prices to come down too much.

Scooter/Motorcycle

Best for... Independent, budget-conscious travellers who like the freedom to travel *Easy Rider* style.

➡ The most inexpensive way to get around.

➡ Available for hire from road-side stalls at beach towns for around 200B a day.

➡ Riding a motorbike on Phuket can be hazardous. Know the risks, wear appropriate clothing and be careful riding at night (see the boxed text, p83).

➡ Alternatively you can find motorbike taxis in Phuket Town, with riders who wear green vests and whom you might con-vince to take you around the island.

Car Hire

Best for... Independent travellers who want to explore the island in depth.

➡ For many, the idea of being behind the wheel in Thailand might seem like madness, but driving in Phuket is a snap. Traffic is manageable, roads are wide and roundabouts are easy to manoeuvre.

➡ Driving is on the left-hand side of the road.

➡ Suzuki jeeps and Toyota sedans go from anywhere from 1200B to 1500B per day (including insurance and GPS).

➡ In low season the rates can come down to 750B. If you hire for a week or more, you'll pay near the low end of the range.

➡ **Pure Car Rent** (☑0 7621 1002; www.purecarrent. com; 75 Th Rassada, Phuket Town) is a reliable company with good rates, as are **Avis** (☑08 9969 8674) and **Hertz** (☑0 2266 4666) at the airport.

Boat

Best for... Those wanting to spend a day island-hopping.

➡ Wooden long-tail boats are the most commonly hired vessel to get to the islands, and are available from many of the beaches.

➡ Rawai is one of the best spots to charter a boat to neighbouring islands – including Ko Bon (1000B), Coral Island (1400B) or Ko Racha (3100B).

➡ From Patong or Kamala, you can head to Freedom Beach, a popular day trip (1800B return). It's also possible to visit Laem Singh and Banana Rock Beach (4200B return).

➡ From Kata, full- and half-day charters head to Coral Island and Ko Bata for around 5000B.

Essential Information

Business Hours

Restaurants Most open for breakfast from around 8am and close at 11pm.

Businesses and shops Open from 8.30am to 6pm in Phuket's Old Town,

and as late as 11pm in resort areas.

Banks Open from 9.30am to 3.30pm Monday to Friday.

Pubs, cafes and bars Open from noon to midnight or later.

7-Elevens Convenience stores open 24 hours.

Discount Cards

Visit in the low season to get 40% to 60% discount on all accommodation, from resorts to backpacker dives.

Electricity

220V/50Hz

220V/50Hz

Emergency

Bangkok Phuket Hospital (☎ 0 7625 4425; Th Yongyok Uthit)

Phuket International Hospital (☎ 0 7624 9400, emergency ☎ 0 7621 0935; Airport Bypass Rd).

Police (☎ 191, 0 7622 3555)

Money

☑ **Top Tip** Don't bother with travellers cheques – they're not worth the hassle, and may not be accepted.

Currency The basic unit of Thai currency is the baht (B), made up of 100 satang. Notes come in 20B, 50B, 100B, 500B and 1000B. Coins are valued at 1B, 5B and 10B. Ask larger vendors or your hotel to break the 1000B notes.

ATMs Theses are everywhere, including the airport, and you won't have any trouble using your ATM or credit cards. It's worth notifying your bank you'll be travelling to Thailand.

Credit cards Widely accepted.

Money changers Also common for those needing to exchange foreign currency, and are also found at the airport.

Tipping Unless there's a service fee already included in the bill, service staff will always appreciate a tip of 5% to 10%.

Public Holidays

New Year's Day
1 January

Chinese New Year
(lunar) January to March

Magha Puja (lunar)
January to March

Chakri Day 6 April

Songkran (lunar) April

Coronation Day 5 May

Visakha Puja (lunar) May

Asalha Puja (lunar) July

Khao Phansa (lunar) July

Queen's Birthday
12 August

Chulalongkorn Day
23 October

King's Birthday
5 December

Constitution Day
10 December

Safe Travel

➡ Considering the number of tourists and the volume of cash spent in Phuket, it's a pretty safe place. You will rarely feel uncomfortable or guarded, even in wild Patong. As in most places in the world, however, violence and crime do happen on the outskirts, especially late at night.

➡ During the monsoon season, the beaches in Phuket are dangerous. An estimated 50 people a year drown because of vicious rip currents on the west-coast beaches. Red flags are posted on beaches when the undercurrents are strong. If they're flying, don't swim in that area. If you do get caught in a rip tide, don't fight it by swimming back to the beach. That's a good way to die. Instead swim parallel to shore. You will eventually elude the rip's grasp. And remember to keep an eye out for jet skis when you're swimming outside the buoys. See the boxed text, p68, for more info.

➡ Also be aware of unscrupulous operators on the main beach areas, particularly Patong. Jet-ski

Money-Saving Tips

The best Phuket deals are available in the low season. Hotels and car-hire agencies routinely slice 50% of their rates in the monsoon season.

➡ There's plenty of cheap and delicious food from street stalls and markets.

➡ Hiring a motorbike or car is the most economical option if you plan on exploring the island.

➡ Prebook your accommodation several months in advance for the best deals.

owners are infamous for scamming tourists into paying for damage to the jet ski's underbody which already existed (see the boxed text, p47). Scooter owners have also been known to try similar things. Making a condition report using your camera will help to avoid any such unpleasantries.

➡ For road safety tips, see the boxed text, p83.

Telephone

Mobile Phones

You can tap into Thailand's mobile phone system in two ways. First, if you have a SIM-unlocked GSM 900-1800 compatible mobile phone, you can simply buy a Thai SIM card and more than one hour of credit for 300B, then pay as you go. Or you can pay roaming rates on your home-country calling plan, which will have a Thai service agreement with a local network. If you do have a Thai SIM card, calling internationally will be cheap and easy and you won't have to use those painful yellow pay phones. Just buy a Phonenet card at 7-Eleven for 300B and call the access number. The call won't drain any of your local phone credit and you can call most countries for 4B to 8B per minute.

Phone Codes

➡ Thailand country code ☎66

➡ Phuket area code ☎076

Useful Numbers

➡ Local directory inquiries ☎1133

➡ International direct dial ☎001

➡ Operator-assisted calls ☎100

Toilets

The bulk of toilets you'll encounter in Phuket will be Western sit-down style, but local places are likely to have squat toilets.

Tourist Information

The **Tourism Authority of Thailand** (☎0 7621 2213; www.tat.or.th; 191 Th Thalang, Phuket Town; ⊙8.30am-4.30pm) is mostly helpful for those interested in Phuket Town, but they have maps and a good selection of brochures for activities on the island.

Dos & Don'ts

➡ The royal family is much beloved, so never disrespect them, which can result in not only causing serious offence, but also in jail time.

➡ Be aware of strict rules for drug possession.

➡ Saving face is an important etiquette and one should avoid public displays of anger or impatience.

➡ Don't point your feet directly at people.

➡ Be sure to always remove your shoes at temples, and dress modestly and cover your shoulders.

➡ Public affection is taboo.

Travellers with Disabilities

Given the narrow footpaths, the pace of traffic and very few adaptations, such as ramps, on the streets of Phuket, travellers with disabilities will have a fairly difficult time getting around by themselves. If you travel with a friend who can help you navigate the chaos on the streets, however, you'll have no trouble at all. If you have disabilities and plan on travelling by yourself, the best bet is to hire a car with a driver who will make sure you get to where you want to go safely.

Visas

Many Western nationals will be granted free entry for 30 days without a visa. See the Ministry of Foreign Affairs Kingdom of Thailand website (www.mfa.go.th) to check whether you must apply for a visa before arriving in Phuket.

Language

In Thai the meaning of a syllable may be altered by means of tones. Standard Thai has five tones: low (eg *bàht*), mid (eg *dee*), falling (eg *mâi*), high (eg *máh*) and rising (eg *săhm*). The range of all five tones is relative to each speaker's vocal range, so there is no fixed 'pitch' intrinsic to the language.

Read our pronunciation guides as if they were English and you'll be understood. The hyphens indicate syllable breaks; some syllables are divided with a dot to help you pronounce compound vowels (eg *mêu·a·rai*). Note that **b** is a hard 'p' sound, almost like a 'b' (eg in 'hip-bag') and **d** is a hard 't' sound, like a sharp 'd' (eg in 'mid-tone').

To enhance your trip with a phrasebook, visit **lonelyplanet.com**. Lonely Planet iPhone phrasebooks are available through the Apple App store.

Basics

Hello.	สวัสดี	sà-wàt-dee
Goodbye.	ลาก่อน	lah gòrn
Yes./No.	ใช่/ไม่	châi/mâi
Please.	ขอ	kŏr
Thank you.	ขอบคุณ	kòrp kun
Excuse me.	ขออภัย	kŏr à-pai
Sorry.	ขอโทษ	kŏr tôht

How are you?
สบายดีไหม — sà-bai dee măi

Fine. And you?
สบายดีครับ/ค่ะ — sà-bai dee kráp/
แล้วคุณล่ะ — kâ láa·ou kun lâ (m/f)

Do you speak English?
คุณพูดภาษา — kun pôot pah-săh
อังกฤษได้ไหม — ang-grìt dâi măi

I don't understand.
ผม/ดิฉันไม่ — pŏm/dì-chăn mâi
เข้าใจ — kôw jai (m/f)

Eating & Drinking

I'd like (the menu), please.
ขอ (รายการ — kŏr (rai gahn
อาหาร) หน่อย — ah-hăhn) nòy

I don't eat ...
ผม/ดิฉัน — pŏm/dì-chăn
ไม่กิน ... — mâi gin ... (m/f)

eggs	ไข่	kài
nuts	ถั่ว	tòo·a
red meat	เนื้อแดง	néu·a daang

That was delicious!
อร่อยมาก — à-ròy mâhk

Cheers!
ไชโย — chai-yoh

Please bring the bill.
ขอบิลหน่อย — kŏr bin nòy

Shopping

I'd like to buy ...
อยากจะซื้อ ... — yàhk jà séu ...

How much is it?
เท่าไร — tôw-rai

That's too expensive.
แพงไป paang bai

Can you lower the price?
ลดราคาได้ไหม lót rah-kah dâi măi

Emergencies

Help! ช่วยด้วย chôo·ay dôo·ay

Go away! ไปให้พ้น bai hâi pón

Call a doctor!
เรียกหมอหน่อย rêe·ak mŏr nòy

Call the police!
เรียกตำรวจหน่อย rêe·ak đam·ròo·at nòy

I'm ill.
ผม/ดิฉัน pŏm/dì-chăn
ป่วย bòo·ay (m/f)

I'm lost.
ผม/ดิฉัน pŏm/dì-chăn
หลงทาง lŏng tahng (m/f)

Where are the toilets?
ห้องน้ำอยู่ที่ไหน hôrng nám yòo têe năi

Time & Numbers

What time is it?
กี่โมงแล้ว gèe mohng láa·ou

morning	เช้า	chów
afternoon	บ่าย	bài
evening	เย็น	yen
yesterday	เมื่อวาน	mêu·a wahn
today	วันนี้	wan née
tomorrow	พรุ่งนี้	prûng née

1	หนึ่ง	nèung
2	สอง	sŏrng
3	สาม	săhm
4	สี่	sèe
5	ห้า	hâh
6	หก	hòk
7	เจ็ด	jèt
8	แปด	bàat
9	เก้า	gôw
10	สิบ	sìp

Transport & Directions

Where's ...?
... อยู่ที่ไหน ... yòo têe năi

What's the address?
ที่อยู่คืออะไร têe yòo keu à-rai

Can you show me (on the map)?
ให้ดู (ในแผนที่) hâi doo (nai păn têe)
ได้ไหม dâi măi

When's the first bus?
รถเมล์คันแรก rót mair kan râak
มาเมื่อไร mah mêu·a rai

A (one-way/return) ticket, please.
ขอตั๋ว (เที่ยว kŏr đŏo·a (têe·o
เดียว/ไปกลับ). dee·o/bai glàp)

Does it stop at ...?
รถจอดที่ ... ไหม rót jòrt têe ... măi

I'd like to get off at ...
ขอลงที่ ... kŏr long têe ...

Index

See also separate subindexes for:

⊗ **Eating** p156

⊙ **Drinking** p157

☆ **Entertainment** p157

🄰 **Shopping** p157

Behind the Scenes

Send Us Your Feedback

We love to hear from travellers – your comments help make our books better. We read every word, and we guarantee that your feedback goes straight to the authors. Visit **lonelyplanet.com/contact** to submit your updates and suggestions.

Note: We may edit, reproduce and incorporate your comments in Lonely Planet products such as guidebooks, websites and digital products, so let us know if you don't want your comments reproduced or your name acknowledged. For a copy of our privacy policy visit lonelyplanet.com/privacy.

Our Readers

Many thanks to the travellers who used the last edition and wrote to us with helpful hints, useful advice and interesting anecdotes.

Author Thanks

Big thanks to Ilaria for giving us a shot at this book and for her assistance throughout. Thanks to Jamie Monk for all his diving info and for running a great Phuket blog. To long-time expat Janzi, thanks for your tips and recommendations. And thanks to the travellers we met who helped with info for our research.

Acknowledgments

Cover photograph: Sunset over Hat Patong, Phuket, Thailand / Jan Wlodarczyk / Alamy

This Book

This 3rd edition of *Pocket Phuket* was researched and written by Trent Holden and Kate Morgan. The previous edition was researched and written by Adam Skolnick. This guidebook was commissioned in Lonely Planet's Melbourne office, and produced by the following:

Commissioning Editors Ilaria Walker, Rebecca Currie **Coordinating Editors** Susan Paterson, Sam Trafford **Coordinating Cartographer** Csanad Csutoros **Coordinating Layout Designer** Carlos Solarte **Managing Editor** Annelies Mertens **Senior Editors** Andi Jones, Martine Power **Managing Cartographer** Diana Von Holdt

Managing Layout Designer Chris Girdler **Assisting Editor** Branislava Vladisavljevic **Cover Research** Naomi Parker **Image Researcher** Aude Vauconsant **Thanks to** Bruce Evans, Ryan Evans, Larissa Frost, Genesys India, Jouve India, Trent Paton, Kirsten Rawlings, Navin Sushil, Gerard Walker

Our Writers

Trent Holden

Having written Lonely Planet books to the neighbouring islands of Sumatra in Indonesia and the Andaman Islands in India, Trent eagerly snapped up the offer to return to research in the paradise that is Phuket. Witnessing first-hand Thailand's changes over the decades, he can happily report Phuket can still turn on charm with the best of 'em, despite its overdevelopment.

Kate Morgan

When Kate first visited Phuket many years ago, you could still get a cheap guesthouse near Kata Noi, Patong was a little wilder and sun loungers were free. While things have changed, she still can't get past how many stunning beaches the island is home to, the charm of Phuket Town or those addictive banana shakes! Kate lives in Melbourne as a freelance writer and editor and has worked on other Lonely Planet books including *Southern Africa*, the *Philippines* and *Japan*.

Published by Lonely Planet Publications Pty Ltd
ABN 36 005 607 983
3rd edition – Jul 2013
ISBN 978 1 74220 037 8

© Lonely Planet 2013   Photographs © as indicated 2013
10 9 8 7 6 5 4 3 2 1
Printed in China